George Orwell

Volume Seven

No. 2

George Orwell

Publishing Office
Abramis Academic
ASK House
Northgate Avenue
Bury St. Edmunds
Suffolk
IP32 6BB
UK

Tel: +44 (0)1284 717884
Fax: +44 (0)1284 717889
Email: info@abramis.co.uk
Web: www.abramis.co.uk

Copyright
All rights reserved. No part of this publication may be reproduced in any material form (including photocopying or storing it in any medium by electronic means, and whether or not transiently or incidentally to some other use of this publication) without the written permission of the copyright owner, except in accordance with the provisions of the Copyright, Designs and Patents Act 1988, or under terms of a licence issued by the Copyright Licensing Agency Ltd, 33-34, Alfred Place, London WC1E 7DP, UK. Applications for the copyright owner's permission to reproduce part of this publication should be addressed to the Publishers.

© 2023 George Orwell Studies & Abramis Academic

ISSN 2399-1267
ISBN 978-1-84549-813-9

Special Tribute Issue to Professor Peter Davison

George Orwell

Contents

Editorial
Peter Davison: A Giant Among Orwell Scholars – by Richard Lance Keeble	Page 3

Tributes
'The *Complete Works*: Clear, Reliable, Scrupulous – and Beautiful' – by Douglas Kerr	Page 8
'Esteemed by Other Orwellians for his Readiness to Offer Help and Encouragement' – by Darcy Moore	Page 9
Farewell & Hail, Peter! – by John Rodden	Page 17
'He Was Nothing if not a Completist!' – by Richard Young	Page 26
How Peter Lives on at Birmingham University – by Nathan Waddell	Page 30
'Peter: My Wonderful, Supportive Friend for 10 years' – by Sylvia Topp	Page 32
'Rather a Great Man' – by D.J. Taylor	Page 36
Why *A Literary Life* is One of the Best Studies of Orwell – by John Newsinger	Page 38
An 'Unparalleled Feat of Respect, Curiosity and Love' – by Dorian Lynskey	Page 41

Articles
Ian Angus's Crucial Role in the Promotion of Orwell Studies – by John Lethbridge	Page 43
Introduction to Publication of Orwell's Original Manuscript for *Nineteen Eighty-Four* – by D.J. Taylor	Page 46
Richard Young on the Original *1984* Manuscript	Page 52
Big Brother Vladimir? – by John Rodden	Page 55

Book reviews
Martin Tyrrell on *Orwell in Cuba: How 1984 came to be Published in Castro's Twilight*, by Frédérick Lavoie (translated by Donald Winkler); Tim Crook on *The Radio Front: The BBC and the Propaganda War 1939-45*, by Ron Bateman	Page 70

Editors
Richard Lance Keeble — University of Lincoln
Tim Crook — Goldsmiths, University of London

Reviews Editor
Megan Faragher — Wright State University

Production Editor
Paul Anderson — University of Essex

Editorial Board
Kristin Bluemel — Monmouth University, New Jersey
Dorian Lynskey — Author, journalist
Peter Marks — University of Sydney
John Newsinger — Bath Spa University
Marina Remy — Paris Sorbonne
John Rodden — University of Texas at Austin
Jean Seaton — University of Westminster
Peter Stansky — Stanford University, US
D. J. Taylor — Author, journalist, biographer of Orwell
Martin Tyrrell — Queen's University, Belfast
Nathan Waddell — University of Birmingham
Florian Zollmann — Newcastle University

With editorial assistance from Marja Giejgo

EDITORIAL

Peter Davison: A Giant Amongst Orwellian Scholars

Tributes to Professor Peter Davison, who died in August last year, form the major part of this special issue of *George Orwell Studies* devoted to his memory. His dedicated editing and annotating – over seventeen years – of the *Complete Works of George Orwell* stands as a towering achievement of academic scholarship. As Douglas Kerr writes in his tribute, it is 'clear, reliable, scrupulous – and beautiful'. Without the publication of the *Complete Works* (totalling more than 8,500 pages) in 1998 it is difficult to imagine the massive growth of Orwell Studies across the globe over the last two decades.

He was esteemed by his students as an outstanding teacher, by his colleagues as an expert on not only Orwell but Shakespeare, Sheridan and the history of English drama – and by other Orwellians for his readiness to offer help and encouragement, as Darcy Moore stresses in his tribute. Indeed, all who came into contact with Peter or corresponded with him found him extraordinarily generous in sharing his profound knowledge of Orwell – the man and his writings. Between 1984 and 2017 he published 31 volumes devoted to Orwell – the last being *A Life in Letters and Diaries* (Folio Society). Its lengthy, autobiographical Introduction was never published – but it was carried over five instalments on The Orwell Society website in 2020. They are crucial reading for anyone curious about the enormous personal (and financial) challenges Peter faced – and overcame. On the *Complete Works*, for instance, he writes:

> My advances totalled just over £12,000 to be earned off by royalties that worked out at £13.75 per £750 set. Out of that I had to pay income tax and most of my working costs (including for example, travel to Caversham several days a week for several weeks) excepting photocopying and postage. When I weighed all the paper at the end of the project it amounted to over half a ton. No one undertakes this kind of edition to enrich oneself but it did mean that journeys I might

RICHARD LANCE KEEBLE

usefully have made – to Barcelona, Huesca, Moscow, the USA or even Jura – were more than I could afford and so were not made. I still have not been to Jura and am now too old to do so.[1]

In this special tribute issue, John Newsinger celebrates one of my favourite Orwellian texts: Peter's *A Literary Life* (1996): it's so elegantly written, concise and packed with insightful gems. Peter also composed a number of important articles (many of them originally written for Dione Venables' *Eric & Us* website and now residing at orwellsociety.com) which should be far better known. For instance, in a piece titled 'Religion and ethical values' (now accessible via the Orwell Foundation website), Peter begins by quoting from Orwell's memoir 'Such, such were the joys' that 'Till the age of about fourteen I believed in God and believed the accounts given of him were true'.[2] By 1917, that year of appalling losses in France, he has given up on Orthodox Christianity. Writing to his friend Eleanor Jaques in 1932, he says he is taking the *Church Times* regularly. How serious or how jokey Orwell is being here has become the subject of some debate. But, according to Peter, soon afterwards 'he quickly developed an antipathy to religious practice, not solely Christianity, especially "political Catholicism" which he likened to Communism as a form of nationalism but also to Buddhism as represented by its young priests who "were the worst of all"'. He ends with a fascinating reflection:

> When Orwell was at St Cyprian's, Wellington (Lent Term 1917) and Eton, on his return to school after each Christmas he would have heard in the first week or two of term the Epistles for the second and third Sundays after Epiphany, St Paul's letter to the Romans, chapter 12, verses 6-21. (In those days the Church of England had more confidence in Cranmer's work than does the hierarchy today and readings were not drawn from all over the place but were firmly set.) I am inclined to think that, whatever he came to believe or not believe, these powerful lessons were a permanent influence on his fighting for the good of mankind.

Another highly original essay focuses on Orwell and sport, covering – amongst other things – his time at Eton (football, cricket, the Wall Game and swimming), his love of field sports and his life-long passion for fishing.[3] Though always a meticulous editor, Peter was self-effacing and (like Orwell) highly self-critical describing himself in his essay 'Getting it right' as 'aware and embarrassed by my multitude of mistakes, misunderstandings, and my sheer ignorance'.[4] He continues:

Orwell's self-criticism of his creative work is well known but possibly not quite so apparent is just how often he corrected the observations he had entered in his diaries. Turning over the pages of his *Diaries* one cannot but be impressed by how often he went back over what he had entered and made later additions, corrections, amplifications, qualifications, and gave vent to his uncertainty.

In his essay, 'Parallel worlds: George Orwell and Vasily Grossman', Peter suggests that hearing John Baker expose the corruption of science under Stalin at the PEN conference in London in August 1944 led Orwell to make a serious start on what was to become *Nineteen Eighty-Four*.[5] Baker focused particularly on the part played by Trofim Denisovic Lysenko who rejected traditional hybridisation and believed he could make wheat become rye. Peter writes: 'Although Lysenko's approach failed utterly he was not discredited in the USSR until 1964. Orwell's writings were frequently attacked, especially by the Communists, but until hearing Baker he believed that science, being "fact-based" was immune from such prejudice.' He goes on to consider the Soviet writer and journalist Vasily Grossman (1905-1964), whose novels, *Life and Fate* and *Everything Flows*, 'show striking parallels' with *Nineteen Eighty-Four* and *Animal Farm*.

> Though neither author knew of the other, nor of what each had written, they saw the dangers of a society destroying genius and denying people their freedom and individuality in similar terms.

Peter lists some of the many similarities between the two authors. For instance, Grossman writes: 'The attitude of the Party leader to any matter, to any film, to any book had to be infused with the spirit of the Party however difficult it might be' while, in *Nineteen Eighty-Four*, 'All the beliefs, habits, tastes, emotions, mental attitudes that characterise our time are really designed to sustain the mystique of the Party and prevent the true nature of present-day society from being perceived.' *Life and Fate* has the story of the proof-reader sent to a labour camp for seven years for missing a typo in Stalin's name. '*Nineteen Eighty-Four* has poor Ampleforth meeting a similar fate for rhyming "rod" with "God".'

And in a remarkable, pioneering essay, of more than 6,400 words, Peter examines in critical detail Orwell's performance at the BBC between 1941 and 1942 and suggests they were far from 'wasted' years, as Orwell maintained.[6]

Running through all of Peter's writings, whether for prestigious book publishers or Orwellian websites, shines his love of scholarship, his enthusiasms and his inspirational determination, as far as

EDITORIAL

possible, 'to get it right'. We are all deeply indebted to him. Thank you, Peter.

- We would also like to thank Peter's sons, John and Hugh, for permitting us to use the wonderful photographs of their father.

*****

Peter Davison was always very keen to stress the important role played by his wife, Sheila, and the librarian Ian Angus in editing the *Complete Works*. It was, in the end, the fruit of a remarkable collaborative venture. Indeed, under the title of each volume run the words, prominently: 'Edited by Peter Davison, assisted by Ian Angus and Sheila Davison.' Yet Angus, who earlier had assisted Orwell's widow, Sonia, in editing the *Collected Essays, Journalism and Letters* (1968), has been sadly forgotten and his death last October, aged 96, went largely unnoticed in the media. Here John Lethbridge brings together the information from his impressive research to provide an appropriately detailed biography of Angus.

*****

One of the major Orwellian events of recent months has been the publication of the *Nineteen Eighty-Four* manuscript by SP Books: Éditions des Saints Pères, of 7 rue Pasteur, 14340 Cambremer, France. Here we carry D.J. Taylor's concise and illuminating Foreword. He highlights one aspect of the novel which has always intrigued me: the role of Winston Smith's secret lover, Julia. I have raised the question in a *GOS* paper (Vol. 4, No. 1: 71-84) of whether she was, in fact, working for the Party and engaged in a honey-trap. It is impossible to say definitively whether she was or wasn't. Orwell deliberately leaves the reader guessing. As I comment in my paper: 'Highlighting the Julia Conundrum (and the question readers are invited to consider: is Julia a spy?) ties in not only with Orwell's epistemological uncertainties and concerns about the growing powers of the secret state – but it also gives the book a strangely modern character, making it a novel about the slippery, unstable nature of meaning' (ibid: 82-83).

In his Foreword, Taylor points out one highly significant cut Orwell is shown to have made. Bidding farewell to Julia, Winston is oppressed by 'a curious feeling that although the purpose for which she had waited was to arrange another meeting, the embrace she had given him was intended as some kind of good-bye'. Here, Orwell clearly thought he was giving too big a clue that Julia was engaged in a honey-trap. Better to leave the question open. So, as the manuscript shows, Orwell cut that section.

*****

Cole Davis, of Volitor, Norwich, whose three collections of Orwell's writings were reviewed in the last issue (Vol. 7, No. 1: 107-111) informs us that they can now be purchased via Gardners.com.

*****

One final point: *George Orwell Studies* seeks the widest range of views on Orwell – the man and his writings. It endorses no particular line or interpretation. All contributors write independently.

NOTES

[1] See https://orwellsociety.com/pete2r-davison-5-regarding-orwell/

[2] See https://www.orwellfoundation.com/the-orwell-foundation/orwell/articles/peter-davison-orwell-religion-and-ethical-values/

[3] See https://orwellsociety.com/orwell-and-sport-by-peter-davison/

[4] See https://orwellsociety.com/wp-content/uploads/2021/04/Jan-Mar-2010-Peter-Davison-Getting-It-Right.pdf

[5] See https://orwellsociety.com/peter-davison-on-orwell-grossman/

[6] See https://orwellsociety.com/orwell-at-the-bbc-two-wasted-years-by-prof-peter-davison/

**Richard Lance Keeble,
University of Lincoln**

TRIBUTE

'The *Complete Works*: Clear, Reliable, Scrupulous – and Beautiful'

DOUGLAS KERR

On my desk lies a volume of *The Complete Prose of T.S. Eliot*, published by Faber and Faber. This edition of eight volumes boasts nine editors; each volume has at least two. In the bookcase at my side stand the twenty volumes of the *Complete Works of George Orwell*. They are the work of a single editor, Peter Davison. The later volumes acknowledge the assistance of Sheila Davison and Ian Angus. I don't make this juxtaposition to sneer at the Faber editors, whose work is exemplary. But I do wonder what possessed Peter Davison to think he could gather and edit Orwell's complete output – and later add *The Lost Orwell* – single-handedly. It seems like the labour of a lost, heroic age.

Political careers, notoriously, always end in failure. The work of academics may linger for a while in the minds of their students – we hope so, at any rate – but their critical writings are all too ephemeral, as tastes and methodologies and fashions change. A scholarly edition is different. Davison's *Orwell* is likely to remain for generations an essential resource for everyone with a serious interest in this author. It is clear, reliable, scrupulous, always well-judged and easy to navigate – a beautiful as well as a useful piece of work. For years I have regarded it – to use a word that publishers are too fond of putting in their book titles – as a companion.

We corresponded a bit, on his part with unfailing generosity and kindness, but I never met Peter Davison. But you get a sense of character from a man's work, and we learned more about him from his published autobiographical writings. I wish I had had the chance to tell him how much I will always respect and admire him.

NOTE ON THE CONTRIBUTOR
Douglas Kerr is the author of *Orwell & Empire* (Oxford University Press, 2022) and of *Wilfred Owen's Voices* (Oxford University Press, 1993), *George Orwell* (Northcote House Publishers, 2003), *Eastern Figures* (Hong Kong University Press, 2008*)* and *Conan Doyle: Writing, Profession and Practice* (Oxford University Press, 2013). He was Professor of English and Dean of Arts at Hong Kong University, and is Honorary Research Fellow at Birkbeck College, London University.

TRIBUTE

'Esteemed by other Orwellians for his readiness to offer help and encouragement'

DARCY MOORE

The late Professor Peter Hobley Davison's academic labour enriched my life. I embarked on the *Complete Works of George Orwell*, the twenty-volumes he edited, in order read the writer's work in chronological order. It became a source of fascination, obsession really, an intellectual adventure of the highest order which contextually transformed my understanding of Orwell and fuelled independent research.

Peter was already advanced in years when I contacted him about this research with a link to my Orwell collection. He politely responded (about five-minutes after I dispatched the email) with the enthusiasm of a bibliophile, saying he was 'amazed' at my 'wonderful, wonderful library'. For the next few years we emailed and discussed Orwell's life and work. Even though he was battling illness, saddened by the loss of his wife, Sheila, and other friends, his intellectual curiosity and generosity of spirit would not be submerged. He provided feedback on papers and articles, 'printing' them off to read 'closely'.

I often told friends and colleagues of this remarkable man and thought it highly improbable my own powers of the intellect, as limited as they might be, would have anything like the longevity that Professor Davison had managed. D. J. Taylor, in his obituary for Peter, accurately described him as a 'a one-man Orwell industry' (Taylor 2022).

A Life in Letters and Diaries, published by the Folio Society in 2017, was his thirty-first and final volume devoted to the work of George Orwell. The first, *Nineteen Eighty-Four: The Facsimile of the Extant Manuscript*, had been published in 1984. Peter was often self-effacing and philosophical in our correspondence but clearly felt a sense of fulfilment knowing how many readers benefited from his scholarship. He once wrote to me saying that:

DARCY MOORE

It really does cheer me that people enjoy and appreciate the edition. I can think of so much I could do better now – but that is life, well, its brevity (Davison 2018: 1 August).

THE ROAD TO ORWELL

Even though my interest was in Orwell, Peter's own life and achievement became a great source of inspiration, especially as it dawned on me that his journey to becoming a phenomenal scholar was a circuitous one. This further enhanced my respect and appreciation of his intellectual achievement. The more I understood, the more it became evident that his life journey was an extraordinary preparation for the monumental task he was to undertake.

Peter left school at 15, during the Second World War, to work in the Crown Film Unit before joining the navy on turning 18. After the war, he returned to the film industry but was sacked by MGM, along with 600 other employees and needed to find alternative employment quickly. Sheila encouraged Peter to apply for a position as a magazine editor, at John Fowler & Co, for which he was unqualified. He gained the position and commenced his career as the editor for *Railways* and the in-house magazine, *Ink*. Peter gained skills which would be invaluable to his future academic career. In particular, a highly-skilled compositor taught him the art of typesetting.

Realising he was only 'superficially qualified' for any job, Peter began a programme of formal education. Sheila, who was a teacher, paid for her husband to take an intensive 10-day Latin course at University College London. He successfully completed A Levels in English, History and Latin. This resulted in better-paid employment.

Between 1952-1960, Peter worked as the assistant secretary and overseas liaison officer to the International Wool Secretariat. During this period he sought a degree in English Literature and studied a wide-range of subjects, including Anglo-Saxon and Middle English, European Drama (1850-1950) and Literary Criticism. John Davison told me that his father:

Navy years.

… reached the secretariat in Lower Regent Street at about 7-7.15 am and could study in peace and quiet in the warmth. for a couple of hours. On the train back home to Burnt Oak he learnt Anglo-Saxon vocabulary and studied the set texts – Beowulf, of course, and a wide range of poetry and prose. He continued to study each evening for a couple of hours and then each weekend (Davison, J. 2022)

Peter and Sheila married on a snowy day in 1949.

Peter continued his studies, taking an MA in Bibliography and Palaeography, at University College London. The skills he developed in deciphering, reading, and dating manuscripts would prove invaluable and lead to further career opportunities. He commenced his PhD, diligently deciphering Elizabethan manuscripts, while continuing to work at the secretariat. In early 1960, Peter called in at the Marlborough Arms where, as expected, he met his supervisor who then unexpectedly asked if he would be interested in an appointment at Sydney University to teach what the department there called 'Scholarship' but was what he regarded as 'Bibliography and Palaeography'. He accepted.

TRIBUTE

THE UNIVERSITY OF SYDNEY

Peter told me that he was drafting 'a longish piece' outlining his life for his children. He mentioned that his wife had written a memoir up until their marriage (which everyone had loved when excerpts were read at her memorial service). Peter shared drafts of his memoirs as he wrote them and it was only then that I realised his connection to Australia. He related some amusing anecdotes about his time in the Antipodes and I discovered he had gained a

DARCY MOORE   PhD in English Literature (Modern Drama), the first awarded by the University of Sydney, in 1963.

Peter Davison with two of his sons in 1963.

When he arrived in Sydney, Peter was expecting to have three months to settle-in and prepare lectures for an introductory course on drama he was to teach. To his 'astonishment' it was expected he begin lecturing for that 'Scholarship' course in just four days' time:

> Had I realised how formidable that class would be – amongst its number were Germaine Greer and Clive James, both far more intellectually distinguished than their alleged teacher – I might have, like their intended teacher, Philip Gaskell, turned tail and shipped the family back to England. But I agreed and I cobbled together what I could and started teaching as proposed (Davison 2018: 12 September).

As Peter, who studied by correspondence, had never given or even attended a university lecture, it was suggested he 'secrete' himself at the back of a theatre and observe one on poetry which should 'provide adequate training'. I flippantly suggested that Greer and James skipped most lectures anyway to write inflammatory articles for *Honi Soit*, the student newspaper, to which he replied:

> I must leap to their defence. They attended well. I did act – well, say a few lines – with Germaine and James asked me to show him a set at Albany when I was secretary. I did remind him he still owed me an essay! It went down quite well (Davison 2018: 12 September).

Peter told me he still corresponded with a lifelong friend from this period, Professor John Bernard (1926-2020), a linguist and seminal figure in the publication of the *Macquarie Dictionary* (see https://www.macquariedictionary.com.au/). J. R. L. Bernard, who went on to become a general editor of the dictionary, wrote a detailed account of the pronunciation of Australian English in a prefatory essay for the first edition, published in 1981. In this year, too, Peter was first to become involved in the intellectual endeavour which was to occupy him for the rest of his life.

Peter's formative academic experiences are extremely significant to understanding what lay at the core of his success as an Orwell scholar. *Nineteen Eighty-Four: The Facsimile of the Extant Manuscript* was the first work on Orwell he published and Peter's explanation as to how this came about is insightful. It was his:

> … ability to transcribe and elucidate the texts in their much over-written Elizabethan hands was what convinced the then-owner of the manuscript drafts of *Nineteen Eighty-Four*, Daniel G. Siegel, that [he] could be trusted to transcribe them for publication in 1984 (Davison 2018: 19 August).

TRIBUTE

Peter working in his study c. 1975.

THE *COMPLETE WORKS OF GEORGE ORWELL* (*CWGO*)

In September 1981, Peter was approached by Tom Rosenthal, of Secker & Warburg, about editing new editions of Orwell's books. Little did he realise at the time the many challenges, scholarly and financial, that he would face (Davison 2012). John Davison puts it nicely:

> It was not meant to be a big task, just a tidying up of previous editions. But, as you know, it didn't turn out like that (Davison, J. 2022: 21 August).

DARCY MOORE

Peter laboured for seventeen years editing, assisted by Sheila Davison and Ian Angus, the *Complete Works of George Orwell*. His attention to detail and eschewment of financial recompense for his hard work, culminated in the publication of the twenty-volume edition, acknowledged by all as a magisterial work of scholarship, in August 1998.

Clive James, himself a wordsmith of repute, admired Peter's achievement in editing *The Complete Works* and it is worth quoting from this former student's review, 'All of Orwell', at length:

> ... if we happened to forget that Orwell himself was a journalist. Here, to help us remember, are the twenty volumes of the new complete edition, cared for with awe-inspiring industry, dedication and judgement by Peter Davison, a scholar based in Leicester, who has spent the last two decades chasing down every single piece of paper his subject ever wrote on and then battling with publishers to persuade them that the accumulated result would supply a demand. The All of Orwell arrives in a cardboard box the size of a piece of check-in luggage: a man in a suitcase. As I write, the books are stacked on my desk, on a chair, on a side table, on the floor. A full, fat eleven of the twenty volumes consist largely of his collected journalism, reproduced in strict chronology along with his broadcasts, letters, memos, diaries, jottings, et exhaustively and fascinatingly al. The nine other volumes, over there near the stereo, were issued previously, in 1986-87, and comprise the individual works he published during his lifetime, including at least two books that directly and undeniably affected history. But, lest we run away with the idea that *Animal Farm* and *Nineteen Eighty-Four* are the core of his achievement, here, finally, is all the incidental writing, to remind us that they were only the outer layer, and could not have existed without what lay inside. Those famous, world-changing novels are just the bark. The journalism is the tree (James 2001: 4).

Even with this success, there were still challenges. John Carey, in a review of what was effectively the 21st volume in the *CWGO*, *The Lost Orwell* (2006), wrote that 'admiration for Orwell quickly forms a bond between perfect strangers, assuring them of each other's inner decency, and it is to this fellowship of loyal Orwellians that Peter Davison's new book owes its existence' (Carey 2006). Secker & Warburg, the original publishers of *Nineteen Eighty-Four* in 1949, although paying handsome sums to celebrities for the rights to publish their experiences in the television series *Big Brother*, could not afford to publish Davison's book. In a letter in my possession, found in an inscribed copy of *The Lost Orwell*, Peter acknowledges to his friends, 'John & Margaret', the help of another Orwellian, David Taylor, to find a publisher, Timewell Press.

VALE PROFESSOR DAVISON

According to John Davison: 'When I think of my father it is not really as an Orwell scholar, but as a Shakespeare scholar with interests in music hall, bibliography and palaeography. Of course, I actually think of him, first and foremost, as a father and family man.'

Professor Davison will be remembered, by most readers, for his work on George Orwell but was justifiably proud of his many years teaching scholarly editing and that the Shakespearean editions he prepared, especially *Henry IV*, stayed so continuously in print. It was only recently I realised that he prepared a critical edition of music-hall songs over half-a-century ago.

The Orwell Society highlighted a quote (in a tweet sent with a link to Professor Davison's obituary) which sums up how we all feel:

> A kind, effusive and unassuming man, he was much esteemed by other Orwellians for his readiness to offer help and encouragement (Twitter 2022).

There are many anecdotes of his intellectual and personal generosity. For example, Dione Venables explained earlier this year, when I visited, her heartfelt appreciation of Peter's support when she was endeavouring to found The Orwell Society.

The last correspondence I received from Peter was on 7 June 2022 while I was staying in Shropshire, at Ticklerton. He told me his eyesight was failing and that writing was near impossible but, as usual, now 95 years of age, he had responded, indefatigable as ever, almost straight away to my email.

I will miss him.

- Special thanks to John Davison for his assistance in answering my questions, providing photographs and generously sharing memories of his father.

REFERENCES

Butler, Susan (1999) The *Macquarie Dictionary*, its history and its editorial practices, *Lexikos*, Vol. 9 pp 152-157. Available online at https://www.academia.edu/81653280/The_Macquarie_Dictionary_its_History_and_its_Editorial_Practices

Carey, John (2006) Insights into a life of genius, *Sunday Times*, 28 May

Davison, John (2022) Email correspondence, August-September

Davison, Peter (1984) Editing Orwell: Eight problems, *The Library*, Vol. 6, No. 3, September pp 217-228

DARCY MOORE

Davison, Peter (2012) The troubled history behind George Orwell's *Complete Works*, *Publisher's Weekly*, 17 August. Available online at https://www.publishersweekly.com/pw/by-topic/industry-news/tip-sheet/article/53594-the-troubled-history-behind-george-orwell-s-complete-works.html

Davison, Peter (2018) Memoirs: shared via email correspondence

James, Clive (2001) All of Orwell, in *Even As We Speak: New Essays 1993-2001*, London: Picador pp 3-24. Available online at *CliveJames.com*, accessed on 8 September 2022

Orwell, George (1998) *The Complete Works of George Orwell*, Davison, Peter (ed.) London: Secker & Warburg

Orwell, George (2006) *The Lost Orwell: Being a Supplement to the Complete Works of George Orwell*, Davison, Peter (ed.) London: Timewell Press

Taylor, D. J. (2022) Peter Davison obituary, *Guardian*, 4 September

Twitter (2022) Available online at https://twitter.com/Orwell_Society/status/1566482976115986434, accessed on 5 September 2022

NOTE ON THE CONTRIBUTOR

Darcy Moore is a deputy principal at a secondary school in New South Wales. He blogs at *darcymoore.net* and his Twitter handle is @Darcy1968. His Orwell Studies Library can be accessed at darcymoore.net/orwell-collection/.

TRIBUTE

Farewell & Hail, Peter!

JOHN RODDEN

THE MAGISTERIAL PETER AND HIS MONUMENTAL ACHIEVEMENT

The passing last 16 August of Peter Davison (1926-2022) was widely and justly memorialised in the literary pages of leading newspapers on both sides of the Atlantic and throughout the English-speaking world. He was certainly no stranger to any reader of this journal: indeed, the names 'George Orwell' and 'Peter Davison' have become practically a collocation during the last thirty years. Rightly so, for Peter became known by millions of readers as the editor of the *Complete Works of George Orwell*, a magnificent tribute to the most influential British writer of the twentieth century. So often have the adjectives 'magisterial' and 'monumental' been applied to this great editorial achievement that they may soon need to be retired, having well-nigh become what the author of 'Politics and the English language' would label 'worn-out metaphors' from overuse. If so, I will find it difficult to find alternatives equally appropriate to describe his feat of editing.[1] For I have acquired very nearly a reflex habit of appending them to the title of this grand edition and referring to it as *The Magisterial, Monumental Complete Works of George Orwell*. (For good measure I would also adjust the title page of each volume to read: 'By the magisterial Peter Davison.')

'IN MY BEGINNING IS MY ENDING'

My title for this tribute alludes to Peter's own parting greeting to the predecessor to The Orwell Society. A dozen years ago, Peter bid 'Farewell & Hail' to the *Eric & Us* Finlay Publisher Archive, the Orwell website (inaugurated by Dione Venables, the reigning elder scholar and doyenne of Orwell studies).[2] Readers of Orwell will recall that, in Jacintha Buddicom's memoir of her friendship with Eric Blair throughout their youth, *Eric & Us* (1974), she mentions that they invoked that greeting of the Roman poet Catullus ('Ave atque vale!') as their parting words from each other:

> 'Farewell and Hail' we adopted as our private salutation, ending 'Farewell and Hail,' so that we should meet again.[3]

Neither Jacintha nor Blair ever forgot their private greeting. In his reply to an unexpected letter from Jacintha, who had written

JOHN RODDEN to him when he lay in Cranham Sanatorium in February 1949, he concludes with a complimentary closing that recalls it – and reflects the extraordinary intimacy they once shared: 'As always ended so that there should be no ending. Farewell and Hail Eric.'[4] I know that many fellow readers and students of Orwell – and of Peter – will join me in saluting this gentle soul and editor extraordinaire: 'Farewell & Hail, Peter Davison! Your passing is not just an ending but also a new beginning.' The debt to the indefatigable Peter Davison for all of us who ponder the life and work of George Orwell is, indeed, incalculable. For our ending is in our beginning, just as our beginning is in our ending – as T.S. Eliot, a poet whom Orwell admired (and knew personally) expressed it.[5]

A RECENT MEMORY

Every person who has spoken to me about Peter has his or her own special memory of the man.[6] Like many people, I first became acquainted with him in the pages of the *Complete Works*, whose early volumes were published in the late-1980s. We later corresponded about Orwell and spoke on the phone whenever I was in London. I also had occasion to talk about him and his work with his friends and contemporaries, such as Ian Angus (the first librarian to direct the Orwell Archive at University College London) and Ian Willison (an early Orwell scholar and erstwhile senior British Library staffer). Like other readers, I followed Peter's feats on behalf of Orwell with a mixture of gratitude and astonishment. They began in his late 50s, when most professors are mulling retirement, with his warm-up, as it were, for the *Complete Works,* his decision to undertake editing *Nineteen Eighty-Four: The Facsimile of the Extant Manuscript* (1984). They continued all the way to the cusp of his turning ninety, culminating in his post-*CW* volume of entries from Orwell's correspondence and journals, *A Life in Letters and Diaries* (2017).

My most intensive, personal contact with Peter, however, came during the last two years of his life, when he asked me to help him revise and introduce a memoir of service during the Second World War in the Crown Film Unit (CFU). At the age of 94, he published a little memoir (with a biographical introduction and a bit of editing by yours truly) in the American journal, *Society*, under the title: 'George Orwell, the movies, wartime England and me.'[7] Peter continued to correspond with people – always replying with an exemplary promptness, a habit cultivated across decades of extraordinary discipline and efficiency as a scholar-critic and editor-bibliographer – but he told me that the wartime memoir would be the last article he would ever write. And that turned out to be the case.

I am certain that any reader of George Orwell would have considered it a privilege, as I did, to work with Peter on that informative memoir. Moreover, the experience was fascinating and edifying for me, for although I was generally familiar with the outlines of his personal history, the memoir was most illuminating about his youth. It provides, therefore, not only a wonderful history lesson addressing a still-obscure part of the war, but also a fascinating glimpse into a previously unknown stage of this scholar-gypsy's strange odyssey, namely his teenage years. As the youngest member of the Crown Film Unit (CFU) during 1942-1944, he began to work 'at the age of fifteen years and nine months', he told me with characteristic precision of detail. He assisted in the production of documentary, dramatic and propaganda films. (Just a year earlier, Orwell, whose writings Peter had already come across, was reviewing films every week for the journal, *Time and Tide*.) For example, Peter worked at the CFU on a feature film, *Close Quarters* (1943), and a number of short films running under ten minutes. He was especially proud of a nine-minute film, *The Eighty Days*, which deals with the V1, the German flying bomb. Snippets of the film still occasionally appear on British television.

At the CFU, he also rubbed shoulders with movie and film stars of the time resident in London. The commercial films on which he worked at MGM brought him into regular contact with many others. For instance, Peter worked on *Edward, My Son* (1949) with Spencer Tracy and Deborah Kerr, and on *The Conspirator* (1949) with Robert Taylor and Elizabeth Taylor. (They were unrelated and never lovers.) The teenage Elizabeth had just appeared on the cover of *Time* after the recent success of *Little Women* (1949), in which she had a prominent role (as Amy March). Peter recalled: 'Elizabeth was then about 17, very beautiful – and charming.' As his thoughts wafted back to that magical moment of his youth as a 22-year-old, he savoured anew the 'pleasure of sitting with her whilst we saw the previous day's film rushes'. Born in London of American parents, Elizabeth had been under contract with MGM when Peter first ran into her during the war in the course of his work at the CFU. Although she had by this time performed minor roles in *Lassie Come Home* (1943), *Jane Eyre* (1943) and *The White Cliffs of Dover* (1944), she was not yet the world-famous screen star she would soon become after the release of *National Velvet* during Christmas week of 1944 – and even more so five years later after *Little Women* and *The Conspirator*. The captivating Elizabeth would sit and chat with him, often sharing a chocolate – a treat not to be had in wartime for an ordinary English bloke.

TRIBUTE

JOHN RODDEN THE UNLIKELY CAREER PATH OF A SCHOLAR-BIBLIOGRAPHER

Peter's journey into the literary academy was certainly unorthodox – yet it seems today in hindsight to have equipped him, at each stage, with valuable skills that informed his scholarship and editing. After his father died when he was just seven years old, he entered an orphanage, then subsequently attended the Royal Masonic School for Boys in Bushey, Hertfordshire, where he became the youngest sergeant in its cadet corps before leaving for the CFU. Rejected by the navy (where his father had served) on account of poor eyesight, Peter joined the Home Guard at the age of 17. ('Sergeant Blair' was also serving at this time in the Home Guard in a different London regiment). Peter also worked on the famous Z Battery, the short-range anti-aircraft weapons system of rocket launchers in Britain's wartime air defence. (It was – signs and wonders! – known as 'the 101'.) In the spring of 1945, he was finally accepted into the navy, served as a radar mechanic and was promoted to petty officer.

This brief outline of Peter's early days evinces that, during his challenging and adventuresome youth, he learned the importance of hard work, resourcefulness and persistence. His story is almost a classic *bildungsroman* – and though he never came into any inheritance, he otherwise could have fittingly called himself an academic version of Dickens's Pip. Demobilised in March 1949, he briefly returned to the CFU before joining MGM as a production assistant later that year. In his CFU memoir, he describes his transition from the CFU to the Home Guard to the navy:

> We then worked five-and-a-half days a week and I was paid 25 shillings a week until I was 16, when my pay rose by five shillings. There was no question of several years' training at university level as nowadays. Indeed, my training lasted all of two weeks. I was instructed in simple tasks such as joining film, filing it away, and finding it again. My instructor, John Reeve, became a very good friend. Indeed, had he not been drafted unexpectedly he would have been best man at my wedding. We both joined the Home Guard, and as there was no real call for two young men trained to fire a Spigot Mortar, we transferred to the aptly numbered 101st 'Z' Rocket Battery near Slough until he was called up to the army and I to the navy.[8]

Peter served mainly in Singapore. Returning to the UK after the war he took up a post again at MGM but in late 1949 was sacked, along with 600 other employees, in a downsizing measure. Marrying just a few weeks later, in December, Peter immediately scrambled to find work. As if gifted with prophetic vision like the author of *Nineteen Eighty-Four*, he began assembling the ideal skillset for the great career that was not yet visible on the horizon. Peter took a job as the editor of the magazine *Railways,* where he learned typesetting as well as gaining valuable experience as an editor-proofreader. Then, in 1952, he became assistant secretary for the International Wool Secretariat, a post he held for eight years. In this new position, he did editorial work and helped mount fashion shows in London, Paris and Athens.

'It was only then that the scholarship bug began to bite,' Peter recalled. He worked full-time and took a correspondence course, first for his school-leaving A-level exams (in order to qualify for university) and then an undergraduate degree at University College London in Bibliography and Palaeography. (The latter field involves training in the dating and deciphering of handwriting, among other aspects of manuscript assessment.) It was in the course of pursuing his Bachelor's and Master's degrees that he first learned to analyse and edit manuscripts. Those skills were further honed during his PhD studies in Australia. Peter elaborated in his memoir:

> I had become interested in New Testament Greek and work in Athens prompted me to take this further. I enrolled for a first (external) degree at London University in English. I graduated by part-time study and the scholarship bug truly bit. I was clearly a late developer! The award of that degree led to a second. I edited a Jacobean play (*The Fair Maid of the Exchange*). This led to the award of an MA and the publication of the play by the Malone Society and the appointment of a lectureship at Sydney University.

Throughout his years in Australia, Peter taught mainly Elizabethan drama. (Among his students were Germaine Greer, Robert Hughes and Clive James.) He learned by doing, having never delivered a lecture before – nor ever even attended a university lecture! Peter had, in fact, never even set foot in a classroom since his first year of high school, given that he had attained his degrees through part-time correspondence courses. His self-designed 'teacher training' was consistent with everything else that characterised this ever-resourceful autodidact. He ensconced himself inconspicuously in lecture halls between his own classes and then imitated the behaviour of his Sydney colleagues in his own classes. (I tremble to imagine facing the likes of Greer, Hughes and James under such conditions.)

Peter worked concurrently, mainly at night, on his PhD, finishing in 1963. This marked yet another trail blazed: he was the first in the university to be awarded a PhD in Modern Drama. Soon afterwards, Peter published an essay on Ben Jonson's *Volpone,* which came to the attention of the head of the Shakespeare Institute in

JOHN RODDEN

Birmingham. So Peter was soon on his way back home to England, thanks to his appointment as a Fellow of the Institute. During the 1960s and 1970s he continued his Shakespeare scholarship and was suitably rewarded, becoming a full professor at Lampeter, later taking up a chair at the University of Kent.

PETER PILGRIM

It is an amazing story. Our pilgrim's progress toward Orwell Studies, therefore, witnesses our high school dropout moving from his CFU and MGM film days into magazine editing, whereupon the lit bug's bite drove him both to undertake a correspondence course to finish school and thereupon to dive into an English degree. After that the bug bit again and he was transported to Australia and tossed into a whirlwind of teaching university courses, pursuing a PhD and eventually landing in Shakespeare Studies as a scholar-bibliographer. During virtually all of his academic career – until he entered his sixties in the mid-1980s – Peter was known as 'a Shakespeare man'. Yet nothing is ever wasted, and the strangest and most decisive episode in his pilgrimage towards Orwell Studies was now at hand. Impressed by his palaeographic work in Elizabethan drama, Daniel G. Siegel, the owner of the manuscript of *Nineteen Eighty-Four,* invited Peter to edit it. Impressed, in turn, by Davison's palaeographic skills with the Orwell manuscript – Peter had to decipher Orwell's handwriting on the extant manuscript pages – publisher Tom Rosenthal at Secker & Warburg contacted him in 1981 to do a 'modest' job of checking over and re-editing Orwell's six novels and three works of nonfiction, which Rosenthal presumed would need to be 'lightly' edited.

It was Peter's big break – and very nearly led to a big breakdown. In the course of scrutinising dozens of earlier editions and other materials, Peter discovered so many errors and inadequacies that the 'modest' job escalated into a seventeen-year labour of love – or tragicomedy of errors. After his meticulous editing and proofing of the first three books, he learned that the printer had mistakenly used the uncorrected proofs to print the books – which had to be pulped. Far worse was that his London and New York publishers abandoned the next volumes in the edition in 1988 – and then again – another *five times* during the following decade. Secker & Warburg pulled out in 1985, then Harcourt Brace Jovanovich, in New York, pulled out in 1993. Then again, they reversed themselves, only to pull out again in 1994 – after 3,188 pages had been typeset and proofread by Peter (with the assistance of his wife, Sheila, and Ian Angus). Suffering heart ailments from all the stress, Peter underwent a sextuple heart bypass a year later in December 1995.[9]

Nevertheless, each setback was merely temporary. He could be slowed but not stopped. Contract or no contract, publisher's commitment or no commitment, he soldiered on. His own commitment was firm, since his tireless labours were for Orwell. Or rather: for Orwell's readers – for us. He stayed on the job, unbroken and unbowed – and prevailed through it all – all 8,150 pages of it.

And never regretted accepting the call to edit Orwell's work.

So it was that Peter embarked in the early 1980s on his second, even more distinguished academic career as the editor of Orwell's *Complete Works*. After countless frustrations and delays, the edition was eventually published, starting in the mid-1980s and continuing through to the late 1990s. When the last volumes finally appeared in August 1998, the raves were legion and the superlatives unending.

Peter with his wife, Sheila, displaying his OBE.

TRIBUTE

An OBE from the Queen for 'Services to Literature' followed in 1999, thus imprinting Peter's career with an official 'magisterial' stamp. (An almost equally splendid honour was his selection to brainstorm the questions for a round of *Mastermind*, the BBC quiz show.[10])

The *Complete Works* were treated as a cause for national pride – and rightly so. In fact, I ask the indulgence of the ghost of George Orwell to permit me, in this one instance, to give his faithful servant Peter top billing at this crucial turn-of-the-century juncture in Orwell's reputation. For if Orwell was the brilliant author whose plain style – 'prose like a windowpane' – made him so wonderfully readable that generations of readers have found his work accessible and inviting, it was nonetheless Peter Davison whose noble scholarly

JOHN RODDEN

crusade made the accessible 'complete' Orwell *truly accessible*. That is to say, Peter made accessible to us readers *all* of Orwell's stunning achievement, placing his long-forgotten or utterly unknown work in scrupulously edited, expertly annotated, attractively designed volumes, selected material from which subsequently became available in economical paperback editions from Penguin during the first decade of the new century.

No longer was a visit to the Orwell Archive the *sine qua non* for Orwell scholars and serious readers who wanted to read more of him. My fellow scholars of Orwell will recall the ancient, hoary days of the late 1970s and early 1980s, when Orwell Studies was still in its infancy and much of Orwell's nonfiction, correspondence and diaries were only available to those who visited the archive. (Nor did the skeletal staff – which in its early years mainly consisted of one man, Ian Angus – have the time or resources to organise and catalogue the holdings. Boxes were simply plunked on my library table by Ian or another staffer, with the instruction to 'go through this' because 'something might be worthwhile here'.)

Peter concluded a short memoir about the 'troubled history' of his saga to complete the *Complete Orwell* with the question: 'To this day, so many of us ask, when facing some new challenge or outrage: "What would George say?"'[11] I am usually skittish about responding to that incessant interrogative posed by media pundits and polemical bloggers, but in this case, I have no doubt. 'Dear old George,' as Peter sometimes referred to him, would have thanked Peter profusely for his painstaking, long-suffering travails – and joked that 'the Davison edition' was not just monumental and magisterial but *doubleplusgood*.

Peter could look back on it with fondness, as if the years of pains accompanying his long-gestating editorial childbirth were simply the high price of the great fulfilment of bringing it to life. As he wrote before his death of his scholarship on Shakespeare:

> One very happy result was an invitation to edit the work of George Orwell and with the help of my dear late wife [Sheila] and Ian Angus, that [labour] was successfully accomplished in some twenty-two volumes.

Yes, it is quite a story – complete with a 'happy' ending. Indeed, it is a *bildungsroman* worthy of a late successor to Pip, a tale of great expectations 'professed' and fulfilled.

And so, let me repeat: Hail & Farewell, Peter! The debt owed to you by all of us who ponder the life and work of George Orwell is incalculable. It cannot be repaid, but only acknowledged – and honoured by building on your work in the same spirit of unflagging persistence and scrupulous integrity that you exemplified.

We are all standing on your broad, strong, multi-volume shoulders!

NOTES

[1] I am not alone in my reliance on those adjectives when it comes to describing Peter's achievement. Jeffrey Meyers opened his review of the *Complete Works* as follows: 'Peter Davison's magisterial edition of Orwell's *Complete Works* includes everything in [Gillian] Fenwick's [recent] bibliography and a great deal of fascinating complementary material'

See *Papers of the Bibliographical Society of America*, Vol. 95, No. 1, 2001 pp 121-24. See also Sam Roberts, Peter Davison, Orwell scholar on a monumental scale, dies at 95, *New York Times*, 15 September 2022. Available online at https://www.nytimes.com/2022/09/15/books/peter-davison-dead.html

[2] Peter Davison, Orwell Society website, 8 November 2011. Available online at https://orwellsociety.com/peter-davison-bids-farewell-hail-to-orwell-site/

[3] *Eric & Us*, second edition, 2006, with postscript by Dione Venables p. 165

[4] George Orwell, *Complete Works*, Vol. XX p. 44

[5] T.S. Eliot's famous line that opens *East Coker*, the second poem of *The Four Quartets*: 'In the beginning is my ending' alludes to the circularity of our life journey, from cradle to grave. And also from grave to cradle

[6] For two other tributes to Peter Davison by close students of his work who write with empathy for and understanding of his life and work, see David Taylor's obituary in the *Guardian*, 4 September 2022. Available online at https://www.theguardian.com/books/2022/sep/04/peter-davison-orwell-scholar-obituary. See also Darcy Moore's moving and richly detailed blog entry, supplemented by family photographs and enriched by interview statements from Peter's son John, in the author's 19 September 2022 blog under the title 'A tribute to Professor Peter Davison'. Available online at https://www.darcymoore.net/2022/09/19/a-tribute-to-professor-peter-davison/

[7] Peter Davison, George Orwell, the movies, wartime England and me, with an Introduction by John Rodden, *Society*, 57 (December 2020) pp 593-595

[8] Ibid p. 594

[9] For Peter's report of the endless pains that he suffered during its gestation, see his The troubled history behind George Orwell's *Complete Works*, *Publisher's Weekly*, 17 August 2012. Available online at https://www.publishersweekly.com/pw/by-topic/industry-news/tip-sheet/article/53594-the-troubled-history-behind-george-orwell-s-complete works.html

[10] On this point, see Ron Bateman's memories of Peter on The Orwell Society website, Peter Davison: A personal memoir, 20 August 2022. Available online at https://orwellsociety.com/peter-davison-a-personal-memoir/

[11] See Davison's The troubled history

NOTE ON THE CONTRIBUTOR

John Rodden is the author, most recently, of *George Orwell: Life and Letters, Legend and Legacy* (Princeton, 2020) and of a forthcoming study, *George Orwell, Plagiarist?*.

TRIBUTE

'He Was Nothing if not a Completist!'

RICHARD YOUNG

I came to know Peter Davison late in his distinguished career as an Orwell scholar. That was a career which lasted for around 40 years, from his first editing work on Orwell's published novels in the early 1980s, right through to a final volume produced for the Folio Society in 2017.

The Folio Society volume was the 31st volume devoted to Orwell which Peter edited or produced. At the core of that work was, of course, the monumental 20-volume *Complete Works*, covering not just Orwell's novels but all the journalism, letters and diaries Peter could locate. This appeared in 1998, following a very difficult path to publication which Peter has described on several occasions. Indeed, so taxing was the effort to get the *Complete Works* to publication that Peter would have been forgiven for calling it a day at that point (especially as he was entering his 70s at the time). But not a bit of it; instead, he periodically edited Orwell volumes for a further 20 years.

I was one of the original subscribers to the new twenty-volume set, which arrived in a large cardboard box, almost too heavy to lift. That set, which cost around £800 I think, now seems to retail (if you can find a set) for more than £2,000. It sits behind me now on the shelf, and has provided endless pleasure and fascination over the years, not the least because of Peter's copious notes, which provide helpful context and background to Orwell's writings.

Peter added a further volume of unpublished Orwell letters and other material to the set in 2006, with a volume called *The Lost Orwell*. However, he continued even then to look for new material which might emerge, however minor. He was nothing if not a completist!

In 2009, I was in touch with D.J. Taylor, Orwell's biographer, about a recent auction sale of Orwell letters written to Orwell's Southwold friends Dennis and Eleanor Collings. Before her 1934 marriage to Dennis, Eleanor had, during the period 1932-1933, been one of Orwell's girlfriends, and they remained in touch even after her marriage to Dennis. I acquired some of the letters – all of which had been published by Peter in the *Collected Works*. There was, however, a rumour that there was a further cache of letters to Eleanor which had been held back from the sale and were unpublished. Both David and Peter were keen to get sight of these letters (in the end these letters were held back for a further 10 years until acquired by Richard Blair from the Collings family for the Orwell archive, and they have now been incorporated as source material into the new Orwell biography from D.J. Taylor which will appear later this year).

I had happened to mention in correspondence with Taylor that I had also acquired at auction that year some proof copies of three of Orwell's 1930s books. Taylor mentioned this to Peter who expressed interest in seeing two of the proofs – *A Clergyman's Daughter* and *Keep the Aspidistra Flying*. I, therefore, got in touch with Peter by email, who promptly invited me to visit his home in Marlborough with the proofs. So it was that on 1 September 2009, I found myself sitting down to lunch with Peter and his wife, Sheila, in their home. Peter was interested in the proofs because both of these early novels had had difficult passages to publication. For various reasons the publisher, Victor Gollancz, had requested a substantial number of changes to the novels before he would publish them. When Peter came to produce new edited versions of these books in the 1980s he had tried to restore the texts as far as possible to the version Orwell had written. As the original manuscripts had not survived, the only source he really had was the correspondence in the Gollancz publishing files. So he was keen to see if there was anything in the proofs which he had missed.

Proofs these days are often produced for promotional purposes, but back in the 1930s they were mainly working documents for publisher and author to refine texts for final publication. Few 1930s book proofs survive as they were typically fragile, paper-bound, uncorrected versions of the text, printed in small quantities and usually discarded once the book was published.

I agreed with Peter that I would go through the proofs, comparing them against the published first editions (which I also had) and finally against the *Collected Works* versions of the text, to see if there were any additional text to be found which Peter had not managed to restore. I did find some changes, and Peter very generously said that we could put the resulting read-out into an appendix in the latest Orwell volume which he was currently working on.

This was a volume called *George Orwell: A Life in Letters*, which largely consisted of a selection taken from the much larger *Collected Works*. Peter was keen to include new material, though, and aside from the unpublished Collings letters, which he was never sadly to see in time to include in any of his volumes, he had found one or two other unpublished letters which he added to the new book. He

TRIBUTE

RICHARD YOUNG

also added my proof read-outs in a separate section entitled 'New Textual Discoveries' on pages 491-92 of the book. In addition, he kindly acknowledged me in respect of his use of some of Eileen Blair's letters, which I also owned, and which he had published previously in the *Lost Orwell*. Interestingly, he told me in an email at the time that he had had a 'great trouble' persuading the publisher of *A Life in Letters* to include any of Eileen's letters. This became a bit of a recurring theme, with publishers much less interested in material from those around Orwell, even when it provided unique insight into the man himself. This was something that frustrated Peter enormously.

I maintained a regular email conversation with Peter over the next few years, and he was certainly very pleased to see The Orwell Society being launched in 2011 (which I soon joined). Peter and Sheila both had mounting health issues over this period, and Peter began to scale back his Orwell work, but I think he found it difficult to let go completely. As such, before too long, he was working on yet another volume. This was to become the 2014 publication *Seeing Things as They Are*. This volume consisted largely of some of the more obscure Orwell journalism, with again much of it taken from the *Collected Works*, and with a new introduction by Peter. Once again Peter was keen to include a new piece of material which I had unearthed. This was a BBC script of a broadcast about Orwell from September 1946 by Daniel George entitled 'The Written Word'. Produced by John Arlott, it was important because, as Peter pointed out, it represented 'the first sustained critical assessment of Orwell's journalism', and certainly the first to be broadcast. It was quite a short piece and obviously had spun off the recent rise in Orwell's prominence with the success of *Animal Farm* (funnily enough, Daniel George had recommended this novel to the publishers, Jonathan Cape, in 1944, but they had rejected it). I had come across the script some years earlier on sale from a bookseller and had bought it for a few pounds. Even in his mid-80s, Peter was still full of enthusiasm for material such as this, and I showed him the script at his house in 2013, followed by a splendid lunch I hosted for Peter and Sheila at their favourite pub near Marlborough.

Peter was determined to add it to his latest volume, and did some further research which confirmed that the BBC also had the script, which had been hidden in their archive, and which matched the version I had provided. Then came the hitch. There was much correspondence between Peter and the publishers during the first part of 2014 about the shape of the new Orwell volume, in terms of the theme particularly. The publishers also wanted a number of items cut from the book, and Peter's original idea of using my script as part of the introduction was shot down. Instead, the publishers wanted to put it in an appendix. In the end, after much discussion and digging in of heels by Peter, a compromise was reached and it appeared in the book in the correct chronological order alongside the chosen items of Orwell's journalism. If you want to read the script you can find it on pages 373-379 of *Seeing Things as They Are*.

Peter's final project was a book for the Folio Society *George Orwell: A Life in Letters and Diaries*. This was largely culled from previous volumes and contained no new items, except for the introduction which Peter wrote, and which was his final published writing, certainly in terms of book appearances (an original plan for a longer biographical introduction by Peter looking back at his life was dropped, though the draft for that can be read on The Orwell Society website).

In 2015, Peter began a clear-out of some of his papers, and he offered me a dozen packed folders of articles and cuttings about Orwell that he had collected over many years, including quite a few relating to the publication and reception of the *Collected Works*. There was also some material which he had used in the preparation of the 20 volumes, including some original letters from people who had known Orwell, like Jon Kimche, Julian Symons and Celia Kirwan. I collected these papers during the summer of 2015, and I am very grateful to have them. As many people will know, Peter donated many of his books, via The Orwell Society, to the Museum of Wigan Life. My intention is that these papers, which Peter was keen to clear and which I enjoy referring to, will also be donated at the appropriate time.

I last saw Peter when he came up to London in the autumn of 2017 for the unveiling of the Orwell statue at Broadcasting House. This was shortly after the death of his wife, Sheila, which was a shattering blow to him.

We stayed in touch after that, never failing to exchange Christmas messages. His last Christmas email to me in December 2021 said: 'Alas, I can do very little but it is good to hear from old friends.' That was both ironic and sad, as Peter was a man who had done so much. All of us who revere the work of George Orwell are truly grateful for Peter's unique and unstinting contribution to Orwell scholarship, and through that work he truly was a friend to all of us.

NOTE ON THE CONTRIBUTOR

Richard Young currently works in the City of London for a financial data company. He is married with one daughter and lives in Epsom, Surrey. He has been a keen Orwell collector for many years and is a member of The Orwell Society.

TRIBUTE

How Peter lives on at Birmingham University

NATHAN WADDELL

I never knew nor met Peter Davison, but I first encountered his work, unwittingly, in 1997. I was studying Orwell's *Animal Farm* for my GCSE exams. The edition we used was a Penguin Modern Classics volume with one of those enticing light green spines. Its front cover was a detail from a painting of some pigs. The text, of course, had been re-established and edited by Peter a decade beforehand, and so it was in a very important sense *his* Orwell I was being taught. I didn't realise then what learning about *Animal Farm* would take me to: a long fascination with Orwell and an obsessive interest in the textual details of his prose.

A very patient auntie, noticing my enthusiasm (and having studied English herself at university), bought me the four-volume *Collected Essays, Journalism and Letters*, which I devoured without really understanding all of it. (I would have been fourteen at the time.) Soon afterwards – this must have been in 1998 – I happened to be in the Cribbs Causeway branch of Waterstone's, in Bristol, where I noticed a line of dark blue hardback books on a high shelf. These were the non-fiction Orwell editions edited by Peter with the assistance of his wife, Sheila, and Ian Angus, running from *A Kind of Compulsion* through to *Our Job is to Make Life Worth Living*. They seemed magical, totemic. I promised myself that one day I'd possess them.

The next time I saw them all lined up on a shelf was in very different circumstances, when I was helping the widow of a much-missed academic mentor to empty his office. They had something of the same aura even there. I confess to feeling melancholically envious of this person's good fortune in having acquired them. Paperback versions now adorn my office, a full set of the hardbacks being far too expensive to procure. I have cause to look at and to use them almost every day. It's never a chore.

Orwell flitted in and out of my life at the University of Birmingham, first as an undergraduate and then as a postgraduate. Writing my undergraduate thesis on Wyndham Lewis and Englishness, I needed to consult volume XI of the *Complete Works*, *Facing Unpleasant Facts*, so that I could read Orwell's review of

Lewis's *The Mysterious Mr Bull* (1938). (Lewis got his own back in *The Writer and the Absolute* (1952), whose final section, 'Orwell, or Two and Two Make Four', idiosyncratically assesses Orwell's achievement.)

Birmingham's main library had some of the *Complete Works* books, but not volume XI. I bought myself a cheap second-hand copy that I managed to find somewhere on the internet. When it arrived its scholarly apparatus amazed me. Evidently a gold standard had been set. I like to think I did Birmingham a favour when – as a PhD student there working on Lewis and some of the other modernists – I requested that the library fill in the missing items in its partial set of the *Complete Works*, which it duly did. (The dust-jackets were removed though, predictably. A shame.) The volumes are still there on the open shelves, much thumbed and highly valued by undergraduates, postgraduates and academic staff alike. Peter lives on, textually, in the institution at which he once lectured, long before my time.

Peter in a relaxed mood.

Having enjoyed my own good fortune and privilege in being able to work in a university English department, I've come to depend on the *Complete Works* for several projects. I'm continually astonished at the breadth and depth of erudition they contain. Douglas Kerr once called Peter a 'heroic' editor, and the epithet seems not only accurate but also inevitably inadequate, given the scale of Peter's accomplishment. The spirit of tribute in the remark still stands, however. Orwell Studies would not exist without these volumes, or without the impetus that Peter's editorial labours gave and still give to the field. We all owe to him the Orwell we read, and the Orwell we have come to understand, in these volumes of unrivalled scholarship.

NOTE ON THE CONTRIBUTOR

Nathan Waddell is an Associate Professor in the Department of English Literature at the University of Birmingham. He recently edited *The Cambridge Companion to Nineteen Eighty-Four* (2020) and the Oxford World's Classics version of Orwell's *A Clergyman's Daughter* (2021).

TRIBUTE

'MY WONDERFUL, SUPPORTIVE FRIEND FOR 10 YEARS'

SYLVIA TOPP

I first contacted Peter Davison about my decision to write a biography of Eileen O'Shaughnessy on 26 October 2011, when he was 85-years-old. David Taylor, whom I visited in the spring of that year, had given me Peter's email address, telling me: 'I'm sure he'll be immensely helpful.' Peter did end up sending me around 75 – sometimes lengthy – emails throughout almost ten years, and he was always an enormous help and support for me as I worked on my book. But it wasn't easy to get him involved at first.

To explain all this, I shall have to go back a few steps. When I began thinking seriously about writing Eileen's biography, in the autumn of 2010, I was a huge fan of George Orwell's work. I had read everything I could find written by him, including the wonderful selections in the four-volume collection that Sonia Orwell had published in 1968. But I knew nothing about the 20-volume *Complete Works of George Orwell* which Peter Davison had spent so many years compiling.

My first thought was to approach Christopher Hitchens with my idea. We worked together at *Vanity Fair* magazine and had become friends years earlier, since we shared a love for George Orwell and had gone together to the 2003 American centennial of Orwell's birth. 'I've long been intrigued with the idea of doing a biography of Eileen O'Shaughnessy,' I wrote to Christopher, adding: 'I've admired everything I've ever read about her, but I haven't been able to find a book about her life. If no one yet has attempted a biography of her, I would love to try.' When he replied: 'I am pretty sure that field is clear: what an excellent idea,' I started taking the project seriously. Christopher added: 'The best man to contact would be D.J. Taylor but I don't know how to reach him: he's my favorite among GO scholars.'

I somehow managed to find an email address for David Taylor, and we talked on the phone in December 2010. He told me that Eileen had been an extraordinarily positive influence on Orwell's life, and assured me that my 'project is a splendid one, and I hope it works out'. At the end of May 2011, I spent a couple of weeks in Newcastle and London doing my first research, and during that time I had lunch with David at his home in Norwich. That's when I first discovered that I could read all of Eileen's letters in Peter Davison's *Complete Works of George Orwell*.

Peter's response to my first email was terribly disappointing. It was a fairly long email, but essentially he told me: 'I am sorry if I am sounding unwelcoming but really I can't manage any more work or visits etc.,' adding: 'I have, at last, after working for 70 years retired and the Orwell Estate has asked Michael Sayeau to take over from me.' He ended his email: 'I am sorry not to be more obliging but I do get bombarded with requests. Yours regretfully, Peter Davison.'

A day later, I got another email from him with Michael Sayeau's address, and the following note from Peter: 'He is an American academic and so will probably be more obliging! Peter Davison.'

Somehow, I sensed a slight dig at my being what he assumed was an American, and so I answered Peter in what I hoped he would appreciate as a clever response: 'Thank you very much Mr Davison. I have emailed Michael Sayeau and will wait to hear back from him. I completely understand your position, being not so young myself! But I think on the whole I prefer British academics with a sense of humor. Best wishes, Sylvia Topp.'

And I immediately received Peter's delightful reply: 'Dear Ms Topp – Nice response! I think all I know about Eileen will be found in the various editions I have edited – some 29 volumes in all. Especially Vols X-XX of the *Complete Works of George Orwell* and in *The Lost Orwell*. The recent compilations (coming out in the USA from Norton) Orwell's *Diaries* and *A Life in Letters* brings together some of this material. Peter.'

And we were on our way to a wonderful ten-year friendship!

Peter immediately passed on my information to Bill Hamilton, who later became my agent, telling me: 'He seemed intrigued that you were researching Eileen.' And, in a longer email the very next day, Peter wrote: 'I really want to stop and hand over my Orwell work, not just for tiredness but because I am at the age of forgetting and it is so easy to miss things now. Thus, I wanted to – should have – told you that I had tried to find out why Eileen went to Chapel Ridding near Windermere in July 1938. I called there but no one had any information about why that might have been. My guess is that there was an old Oxford Friend living there but I failed to trace anything.'

I understood this to be an assignment for me. And I did finally visit Chapel Ridding and Windermere, in June 2014, and was pleased to discover a few possible reasons for Eileen's visit there in the summer of 1938. Peter kindly credited me with these discoveries

TRIBUTE

SYLVIA TOPP

in his wonderful Preface to my biography of Eileen, one of the last writing assignments he undertook.

We had a lot of adventures along the way. In June 2012, Peter and I discovered a surprise *Vanity Fair* connection. Although Christopher Hitchens was no longer writing a monthly column, having died in December 2011, the magazine was preparing a final column by him that month. As I was editing this piece, I was excited to discover that it was a copy of Christopher's Introduction to Peter's latest book, a collection of Orwell's *Diaries*. I informed Peter, writing: 'Strange how small some worlds are!' And Peter responded: 'It is remarkable isn't it that you should be involved on two fronts as it were!'

Tom Mayer was Peter's editor at Norton at the time, and Peter kindly suggested that he give me a contract for my biography of Eileen. Mr Mayer began his reply: 'Congratulations to you on all of this superb research and putting it together in such a clear and engaging way. I very much enjoyed your sample chapter.' But, alas, after this initial encouragement, he concluded, long before I had written any further chapters: 'The material, as I'm sure you've discovered, is scant. Very few letters survive, and there isn't much in the records.' He was not interested.

Another time, when I asked Peter whether he was 'the Peter Davison who hung out with Sylvia Plath back in the days,' he answered: 'Alas no! I have never walked in such exalted circles!' But he told me that he had often been confused with another Peter Davison, an actor. 'I have just been paid £445 by the BBC for a repeat broadcast,' he wrote. 'It was not mine though and I've had no success yet in getting them to take it back!! It was for 2 two-minute replays of a *Dr Who* broadcast for the actor, Peter Davison! The most the BBC has ever paid me is £30 for a 30-minute World Service broadcast. What a financial contrast!'

From the very beginning, and throughout the ten years, Peter continued to encourage me. He strongly agreed with me that Eileen's importance to Orwell had never been fully credited. In one email, he wrote: 'I am not particularly political but have long thought women – wives esp. – have been under recognised.' In another, he said: 'I do wish you all the best with your book. It will be a really worthwhile addition to the Orwell story. We know far too little about Eileen and she deserves so much more.' Early on, he had confided to me: 'There is so little on Eileen – and, though you had better not repeat it! – the publishers were very averse to my including Eileen's letters!, hard to believe isn't it?'

When my book was finally being published in the spring of 2018, I sent an email to Peter titled: 'A request you can refuse.' In it, I brazenly asked Peter if he would consider writing a preface for my book. I added: 'You have told me many times that you don't feel up to writing much anymore, so I will completely understand if this is an idea you choose to reject. However, I am presenting it in the great hope that you might make one exception. It could be very short, but you, of all the Orwell experts, realize how important Eileen was to him. I remember your telling me that your editors of the complete Orwell collection did not want to include Eileen's letters!! But you insisted.' And I was thrilled when Peter accepted.

However, as he told me: 'I am doing a very different kind of intro – I hope it will properly recognise your achievement – but I am doing it in an unusual way.' And, of course, he went on to compare the help he got from his wife Sheila to the help Orwell received from Eileen, as well as enlarging on the story of his insisting that Eileen's letters be included in the *Complete Works*.

And in a very lovely letter, one of the very last I received from Peter, he wrote: 'Your book has just arrived and it comes in a week in which three friends – two very close – have died. I find reading a slow procedure these days but your wonderful work has Bucked me up enormously. Thank you so much. Yours with love and thanks. A wonderful surprise! Thank you so much. Peter.'

Regretfully, I never managed to meet Peter in person. Through those ten years of emails, he constantly confided details about his wife Sheila's slow deterioration, as he spent many hours a day taking care of her by himself. This important occupation, however, did not seem to stop him from immediately attempting to answer any questions about Eileen that I came up with. I shall be forever grateful that Peter, even though he needed a small amount of persuasion, did agree to take my project seriously at the very beginning of my research. I could never have managed to write such a detailed celebration of Eileen's importance to George Orwell without Peter's continuous help.

NOTE ON THE CONTRIBUTOR

Sylvia Topp is presently working on an article that will focus, for the first time, on Eileen's great influence on Orwell's writing style, as well as emphasising her importance on his developing political and psychological views. She would appreciate hearing from others on this theory. Sylvia is also continuing work on a memoir of her own adventure-full life, anxious to finish it before she forgets any more details.

TRIBUTE

'Rather A Great Man'

D.J. TAYLOR

Although I didn't meet Peter until the early 2000s, I knew about his activities long years back. My first novel was published by Secker & Warburg in 1986 – these were the days when Secker was still a free-standing firm with two dozen employees and an address in Soho – and even then people talked in hushed voices of this legendary figure and the work he was doing in getting new editions of Orwell's novels ready for the printer. The receipt – *gratis*, mercifully, as a reviewer's perk – of the twenty-volume *Complete Works* in 1998 confirmed everything I'd been told a decade before. Here, clearly, was an editor of genius, fit to be compared to Ernest Mehew on Stevenson, Gordon N. Ray on Thackeray or Pierre Coustillas on Gissing, someone whose absorption in their subject meant that they lived and breathed him, retired for the night with his shadow hanging over the bedpost and woke up in the morning to greet him again at the breakfast table.

To start my work on *Orwell: The Life* (2003) was to be thrown into the orbit of senior players in the Orwell game, whose co-operation couldn't necessarily be taken for granted. But Peter, once we had sat down for the first time in his Albany flat, was an inspiration. For the next two years the post brought regular instalments of vital data – the phone numbers of old Orwell cronies, off-prints of scholarly articles that I might have missed, reports from the professional coal-face headed: 'For Your Eyes Only', learned speculations and helpful hints, all imparted as if we were equals, rather than the world's greatest Orwell scholar beaming down from Olympus upon the occupant of a subsidiary crag. What I always remember, and cherish, about Peter was his enthusiasm. If (as I once did) you rang him up from a call box in St Giles, Oxford, on a Sunday morning to convey some choice scrap of Orwelliana just communicated to you by the member of a literary festival audience, he would give you the impression that he had been sitting there in his study awaiting your call and that only duty to his family was stopping him from jumping into his car and driving to Oxford on the spot.

The tribulations Peter went through while compiling the *Complete Works* are well-known: they included a sextuple heart bypass and the project being cancelled several times by timid publishers. After an obituary appeared in the *Guardian* detailing some of these misfortunes, the journalist Richard Williams tweeted the relevant passage with the comment: 'I shall never complain about anything again.' Naturally, it didn't help that he lived in Britain. Any foreign scholar who had done what he did would have been showered with awards and given a personal chair and a team of research assistants to do his bidding. Peter, though nobly supported by his wife Sheila, laboured on his own and made do with an OBE.

Not, of course, that he cared much about this. He was a modest, self-effacing man who avoided the limelight and seemed more interested in the forward march of Orwell Studies rather than reminders that Orwell Studies in their present form would scarcely exist without his contribution. I last saw him at the unveiling of the Orwell Statue outside Broadcasting House, deeply upset by Sheila's recent death but as zealously absorbed in Orwell matters as ever. Orwell's friend Anthony Powell, always sparing of his praise, would occasionally allow that such-and-such a stratospherically distinguished contemporary was 'rather a great man'. Well, take it from me, Peter Davison was rather a great man.

NOTE ON THE CONTRIBUTOR

D.J. Taylor's *Orwell: The New Life* (London: Constable) is to be published on 25 May.

TRIBUTE

Why *A Literary Life* is One of the Best Studies of Orwell

JOHN NEWSINGER

Peter Davison will, of course, be best remembered for his twenty-volume edition of the *Complete Works of George Orwell*. This was one of the great publishing events of recent years. It was a monumental achievement for which scholars and admirers of Orwell and of his writings, both academic and non-academic, will be forever in his debt. But he was also the author of one of the best studies of Orwell, *George Orwell: A Literary Life*, first published in 1996, a book that has never received the attention it deserves. Obviously, his *Literary Life*, less than 200 pages long, was inevitably overshadowed by the publication of the twenty-volume *Complete Works*, but it is still worth revisiting.

In his Introduction to the book, Davison makes absolutely clear that he is 'chiefly concerned with what influenced Orwell – people, reading, circumstances – and his relationship with publishers and editors' (p. ix). This certainly had a big influence on the way in which I came to approach Orwell and his writings. Davison goes on in his Introduction to recount the problems he encountered over the publication of the *Complete Works* with the publisher, Harcourt, Brace, withdrawing from the contract 'without telling the editor' but with Secker & Warburg thankfully stepping in (p. x). As he put it, the *Complete Works* raised Orwell scholarship to a new level: '… close examination of every word Orwell wrote, every event and person referred to has thrown new insights into George Orwell'. He singles out a number of particular insights: '… the true significance of censorship of his work as a writer and as a broadcaster; the importance of the pamphlets he collected in shaping his political ideas', among many others. And there are more specific episodes; for example, 'how his and Arthur Koestler's efforts to reveal the slaughter of Polish prisoners by the Soviets failed to find a publisher'. One of the most significant items, however, was, as far as Davison was concerned, 'the analysis of the deposition laid before the Tribunal at Valencia in 1937 charging Orwell and his wife with Espionage and High Treason, a document which, though he never knew it existed, explains vividly how he came to write *Animal Farm* and *Nineteen Eighty-Four*' (p. xi).

There is so much packed into the pages of *George Orwell: A Literary Life* so I will just indulge myself with regard to some of the discussion that I found most interesting. The account of the difficulties Orwell had in publishing *Burmese Days* and the book's subsequent sales history still fascinate. Gollancz printed 3,180 copies with none being remaindered. Then in May 1944, Penguin Books published a new cheap 9p. edition, '60,000 copies, all of which were sold' (p. 49). Davison's whole discussion of *Burmese Days* which extends way beyond its publishing history is essential reading. He draws on the work of Maung Htin Aung to discuss how comparatively well-paid Orwell had been when serving as a police officer in Burma and how only 'when he joined the BBC and was paid £640 a year, would he approach anything like his Police salary' (pp 15-16).

Then there is his dispute with Bernard Crick, a clash of the Titans, over how much Orwell was advanced for *The Road to Wigan Pier*. Crick posited that Orwell had been given a £500 advance for *The Road to Wigan Pier* by the publisher Victor Gollancz. As Davison writes, '£500 would have been a great deal of money in 1936 and, had Orwell received that, there might be some justification for those who see him as being richly paid to poke into the affairs of those living in poverty'. Davison convincingly argues that this was just not the case: 'Gollancz was far too sensible a man to make such a foolish bargain. Indeed, even after the sale of all the hardback copies and some 44,000 copies of the full edition to members of the Left Book Club, Orwell's receipt from royalties was just under £600 after paying his agent's commission' (pp 67-68). As Orwell's Wigan diary shows, he was frequently short of money while researching and writing the book.

As for *Homage to Catalonia*, Gollancz, of course, rejected it unseen because of its author's politics and Secker & Warburg printed only 1,500 copies, many of which were destroyed in an air raid during the Second World War. The book in Fredric Warburg's words, 'caused barely a ripple', such was the strength of Popular Front sympathies on the Left at the time (p. 86). As Davison insists, *Homage to Catalonia* reveals 'a learning process presented in such a way that the reader is taken through the experiences described' (p. 81). This is one of its great strengths. While the book may have made a negligible impact when first published, as Davison points out, it is today, to the dismay of ageing communists and their sympathisers, 'perhaps the only book still read from that period for a personal and passionate account of the Spanish experience' (p. 144).

TRIBUTE

JOHN NEWSINGER

In his Conclusion, Davison praises *Down and Out in Paris and London* and *A Clergyman's Daughter*, 'which for all their structural infelicities, convey the experience of poverty vividly, and so long as we have people sleeping in doorways, which seemingly will be forever, that remains important' (p. 144). This was true in 1996 and is even more true today. Similarly with regard to *Nineteen Eighty-Four* of which he writes: 'I wish its warnings were no longer necessary. It is not a book I warm to because its warning is a reminder of the blight that may affect our futures and those of our children' (pp 144-145). Once again, even more true today. *George Orwell: A Literary Life* remains essential reading.

NOTE ON THE CONTRIBUTOR

John Newsinger is a retired academic. He is the author of *Orwell's Politics* and of *Hope Lies in the Proles: George Orwell and the Left*. His most recent book is *Chosen by God: Donald Trump, the Christian Right and American Capitalism*.

TRIBUTE

An 'unparalleled feat of respect, curiosity and love'

DORIAN LYNSKEY

It is customary for an author to limit acknowledgements to people they have actually met and who actively contributed to the book but I am not sure anyone was as essential to my writing of *The Ministry of Truth: A Biography of George Orwell's 1984* as Peter Davison. Much though I enjoyed my time in the Orwell Archive, I thought countless times of how much harder the task would have been if Davison had not spent decades collating and contextualising every scrap of Orwell's output. I am sure other contributors will explain the incredible labour and dedication that was required to assemble the *Complete Works* despite numerous setbacks. I will just say that every Orwell scholar must be profoundly grateful for the work that Davison did on their behalf.

It is a tall order for anyone to read two million words by one writer, many of which were never intended for publication, but for those who do, the *Complete Works* is the closest one can come to being able to read Orwell's mind. A classic, oft-quoted essay takes on new meaning when it is surrounded by reading journals, gardening diaries, letters to friends and very relatable complaints about late payments. You can track the evolution of every idea and see something new in every famous line. For my purposes, attempting to establish the origins of all the essential notions and phrases in *Nineteen Eighty-Four*, invaluable is too mild a word.

Given Orwell's strong opinions about what was worth republishing and what should be memory-holed, I suspect

Peter with his wife, Sheila, on his becoming an Emeritus Professor.

DORIAN LYNSKEY

that he would have been mortified to see so much hackwork and ephemera given equal billing with his finest prose but Davison's completism humanises the man like nothing else, cracking open the imposing shell of the prophet, sage and saint and letting us see the prickly, contradictory individual whose brilliance emerged from the everyday business of marriage, friendship, illness, loss and simply trying to pay the bills. The truth is in the mess, not the masterpieces. This full portrait of Orwell would not exist, at least not in an accessible form, without Davison's unparalleled feat of respect, curiosity and love.

NOTE ON THE CONTRIBUTOR

Dorian Lynskey is a journalist, podcaster and author of books including *The Ministry of Truth: A Biography of George Orwell's* 1984.

Ian Angus's Crucial Role in the Promotion of Orwell Studies

John Lethbridge

Ian Angus, who played a key role in the promotion of Orwell Studies through his editing with Sonia Orwell the four volumes of his *Collected Essays, Journalism and Letters* (1968) and later helping Peter Davison in editing the *Complete Works*, has died aged 96. Angus was also involved in the setting up of the Orwell Archive at University College London after Orwell's writings were given to UCL on permanent loan by his widow on behalf of the Orwell Archive Trust in 1960. Orwell's biographer D.J. Taylor paid this tribute:

> Through no fault of his own, Ian Angus is one of the (comparatively) forgotten men of Orwell scholarship. With the twenty volumes of Peter Davison's edition of the *Complete Works* (plus addenda) on the shelf before them, Orwellians tend to forget the existence of the four-volume *Collected Journalism, Essays and Letters* (*CJEL*) which Ian, then librarian of King's College, London, together with Orwell's widow Sonia, edited for Secker & Warburg for publication in 1968. But for those of us who discovered Orwell as schoolchildren in the late 1970s *CJEL* – by this time available as cheap Penguins – was a cornucopia of delight. For good measure, Ian then gave invaluable help to Davison as the *Complete Works* took shape in the early 1990s.
>
> A reserved yet engaging character, Ian was also a great friend to Orwell biographers, always happy to answer questions and offer promising leads, and not averse to intervening in Orwell controversies, as in the correspondence printed in the *London Review of Books* following publication of Michael Shelden's 1991 biography. After I had finished *Orwell: The Life* (2003) he presented me with two priceless Orwell artefacts – the tie given by Sonia to the dying man at Christmas 1949 (now in the Orwell Archive) and two silver gravy boats that Orwell and his first wife Eileen had received as wedding gifts in 1936

JOHN LETHBRIDGE

(now in the possession of Richard Blair.) It was typical of the generosity and self-effacement he brought to over a half century's involvement in Orwell Studies.

Ian Donald Angus was born on 10 May 1926 at 1 Maldon Crescent, St Pancras, London. His parents were Ivan Archibald, a restaurant waiter, and Margaret Emily, née Saunders. At Battersea Grammar School, in the autumn of 1944, he won a £60 open scholarship to study History at Jesus College, Cambridge.

In August and September 1944, he took a short Arts/History course at the college before joining the Royal Navy where he served until February 1947. On 10 November 1945, he was promoted to being a temporary sub lieutenant – a rank equivalent to first lieutenant in the army. He served at *HMS Duke*, in Great Malvern, a shore establishment or 'stone frigate'. According to Ben Marlow's *Shore Establishments of the Royal Navy* (2002), it trained new entry stokers.

According to Jacqueline Cox, of Cambridge University Archives, Ian Angus returned to Jesus College, Cambridge, in the Lent term of 1947, to study for the Historical Tripos. In the Easter term of 1948, he sat Part I of the Historical Tripos and gained an upper second. He then switched to the English Tripos and in Easter term 1949 achieved a lower second BA degree.

THE LIBRARIAN

After graduating, Angus studied at UCL Library School, gaining a 2nd in Cataloguing and Classification, a 1st in General Bibliography, a 2nd in Book Selection and Reference Bibliography, a 2nd in General Library Administration, a 3rd in Elementary English Palaeography, a 3rd in Special Library Administration and a 1st in Historical Bibliography. He passed the third and final part of the course in 1952 gaining a 1st in Bibliography and being awarded a Diploma of Librarianship.

He was appointed an assistant librarian at UCL Library in February 1952 and was responsible for four departments – architecture, town planning, anthropology and librarianship. In September 1956, he was given charge of the history and political economy department.

In August 1958, he was transferred to the library's order and accessions department. That year, he was awarded a Cambridge MA – an honorary degree. It gave him a seat on the Cambridge University Senate and privileged access to Cambridge University Library.

The Orwell Archive was deposited at UCL Library in 1960. To quote a reference from J. W. Scott, the UCL librarian: 'Angus has been entirely responsible for its administration and development.

He has now written to almost every individual who was known to Orwell in an attempt to increase the steady flow of additions to this archive' (6 January 2023, email from Robert Winckworth, of UCL).

In 1964, Angus was promoted to the post of UCL deputy librarian. Four years later, his collaboration with Orwell's widow, Sonia, led to the publication of the four-volume *Collected Essays, Journalism and Letters* by Secker & Warburg (now Harvill Secker). He went on to assist Peter and Sheila Davison in the editing of the monumental, twenty-volume *Complete Works*. Angus was appointed librarian of UCL's King's College Library in 1975, holding this position until he retired in 1982.

PRIVATE LIFE

On 18 September 1976, Angus married Ann Stokes, a ceramics artist and widow, aged 53, of 20 Church Row, Hampstead. She was the daughter of a Church of Scotland minister. The service was held at Hampstead Registry Office. After the marriage, the couple lived at 20 Church Row, Hampstead, a Georgian house once lived in by the architect Thomas Garner. Hampstead was not then as expensive an area as it is today but it was already a prestigious area, popular with intellectuals.

Ann's first husband, the writer and painter Adrian Durham Stokes, had died of cancer aged 70 in 1972. Their son, Philip David, was born in 1948 while their daughter, Ariadne, was born three years later. Stokes's first marriage to Margaret (née Mellis) had been a stormy one and they had divorced in 1947, Margaret later marrying the poet and artist Francis Douglas Davison.

In his retirement, Ian Angus lived for part of the year in Hampstead and the rest in Italy. Ann Angus died of pneumonia at the Royal Free Hospital in Camden on 21 April 2014 aged 91 while Ian died on 30 October 2022 at 20 Church Row, Hampstead.

NOTE ON THE CONTRIBUTOR

John Lethbridge was born in 1959 and studied at Saltley Grammar School and Lampeter, then a college of the University of Wales, graduating in History in 1981. Since then, he has had two books published and has self-published one book and seven pamphlets. He has had many articles published in various journals. His *Foul Deeds and Suspicious Deaths in Warwickshire* was published by Wharncliffe in 2007 and is still in print.

ARTICLE

Publication of *1984* Manuscript

The manuscript of George Orwell's *Nineteen Eighty-Four* has been published by SP Books: Éditions des Saints Pères, of 7 rue Pasteur, 14340 Cambremer, France. The company was founded in Saint-Germain-des-Prés by young publishers Jessica Nelson and Nicolas Tretiakow 'with the aim of creating a unique collection of great manuscripts' (see https://www.spbooks.com/). Here, with the kind permission of the publishers, we carry D.J. Taylor's Foreword.

One morning in the spring of 1950 a young woman left her flat in Percy Street, central London, and set off for the west of Scotland. Her name was Sonia Orwell and her destination was Barnhill farmhouse on the remote Inner Hebridean island of Jura where her husband had spent much of the last four years of his life before dying in University College Hospital a few months before. The journey was an arduous one, and the instructions given in a letter George Orwell wrote to her in 1947 proposing a visit run to 19 lines of type: a train to Glasgow; a second train to the coast; a ferry-ride from the mainland; a punishing drive over poor terrain to the island's northernmost tip. Sonia is unlikely to have accomplished it in less than a day and a half. Her primary aim was to inventory the effects that Orwell had left there before his departure at the end of 1948 and decide what needed to be done with them, but you imagine that she would also have been driven by straightforward curiosity. This, after all, was the place where her husband had spent his declining years, as tuberculosis continued to ravage his lungs and he struggled to complete his final work, the prodigiously best-selling *Nineteen Eighty-Four* (1949). What would she find there?

One thing Sonia did turn up, in the bleak, draughty bedroom which Orwell had used as a study, was a large pile of manuscript. Some of it was written in biro; other pages, much corrected and scored over, clearly came from Orwell's typewriter. Sonia, assuming that this was the original of *Nineteen Eighty-Four*, took the material back to London. Here in the 1950s, much less fuss was made of literary leavings, and Sonia seems not to have known what to do with her find. In the end she donated it to a charity auction, in much the same way that, a decade later, she would bestow the machine on which Orwell had typed it to the radical newspaper *International Times*. Bought by Scribner's of New York for what now seems the bargain price of £50 ($140), the lot was sold on to a private collector in Kansas for $275 – slightly under £100 in English money – and then, in 1969, purchased by Daniel Siegel for $5000. Fifteen years later, edited by the distinguished Orwell scholar Professor Peter Davison, it would form the basis of *George Orwell: Nineteen Eighty-Four: The Facsimile of the Extant Manuscript: With a Preface by Daniel G. Siegel*.

Sonia, while allowing that her husband was 'not a very good manuscript keeper', had also assumed that the version of *Nineteen Eighty-Four* she had found on the study desk in Jura was complete, and that its contents would more or less correspond with the printed version of the novel issued by Secker & Warburg in June 1949. In fact, she was mistaken about this. Only about 40 per cent of the final text survives, and what remains derives from four different sources. To begin with there are 13 pages of the draft that we know Orwell to have begun in the summer of 1945 and to have worked on while he was staying on Jura in the summer of 1946. To this can be added another nine pages of a redraft from the following year. A single page survives from a version typed by Mrs Miranda Christen, a professional stenographer whom Orwell frequently employed in the mid-to-late 1940s and to whom he sub-let his Islington flat while he was living in Scotland. The remainder belongs to the final, revised version that Orwell produced in the autumn of 1948 when, racked with pain, he laboured to complete the book before his health gave out and he was taken south to what effectively became his death-bed.

All this makes the manuscript of *Nineteen Eighty-Four* a very curious piece of work: incomplete, chaotic and oddly provisional. As such, it reflects the highly unusual conditions in which it was written. One of the great mysteries surrounding the novel's composition is why it took so long to complete. In normal circumstances, Orwell was a fast worker. None of his previous five novels had taken him longer than a year to write, once he had got going, and *Animal Farm* (1945) – only 40,000 words, admittedly, but tricky to schematise in terms of its historical grounding – occupied him for a bare three months. *Nineteen Eighty-Four*, on the other hand, took five-and-half years from the moment of conception – as long ago as the Tehran Conference of November 1943 in which Roosevelt, Stalin and Churchill sat down to carve up the post-war world – to its appearance in hard covers, and seems to have moved forward an inch at a time: a few pages done in the summer of 1945; a more sustained assault in the summer of 1946; more work the following

D. J. TAYLOR

year; the final, strength-sapping engagement of late 1948. What stayed Orwell's hand? One of the most obvious explanations is a crisis – or rather several crises – in Orwell's personal life. His first wife, Eileen, had died unexpectedly in the spring of 1945, leaving him in charge of their adopted son Richard, then only a year old, whom Orwell was determined to raise himself. As well as being a mother to their child, Eileen had also acted as a professional helpmate (for further details see Sylvia Topp's excellent biography *Eileen: The Making of George Orwell*, 2020): in her absence he fell apart emotionally and spent the winter of 1945-6 proposing marriage practically on the spot to any remotely eligible girl he met. Not only did this emotional set-back coincide with a serious decline in his health – his tubercular lung hemorrhaged early in 1946 and he kept out of hospital only by deceiving his doctor – but it ran together with the fulfilment of a long-planned scheme to uproot himself from London and retreat to the Hebridean island where he could bring up Richard, grow plants in his garden and get on with his work in what he assumed would be conditions of absolute tranquillity.

Ill, emotionally bereft, thoroughly exhausted – as were most British people – by the strains of a six-year war, relocated to a new life in the west of Scotland (although he would spend the freezing winter of 1946-7 back in Islington), Orwell was in no state to start work on so ambitious a project as *Nineteen Eighty-Four*. In many ways, though, the problem was worse than this. Anxious as he may have been to set out his vision of a nightmare dystopian future that had its roots in the post-war world he saw around him, Orwell, it soon becomes clear, had yet to establish much of the intellectual topsoil in which the novel's seeds are sown. To examine some of the journalism he produced in the post-1945 period is immediately to appreciate the time he spent rehearsing some of the arguments of the novel, canvassing ideas that would resurface in the world of Airstrip One and the Ministry of Truth. Much more so than any of his previous books, *Nineteen Eighty-Four* is a kind of backward-facing drill that burrows deep into earlier outings and, sometimes subconsciously, turns up all manner of details that will prove to be useful in the task ahead.

One might note, for example, 'You and the Atom Bomb', an essay published in the left-wing weekly magazine *Tribune* in October 1945, a bare two months after the nuclear warheads had obliterated Hiroshima and Nagasaki. Here Orwell maps out a geo-political future in which the world is divided into three great land-masses, oligarch-controlled and permanently at odds with each other, indefinitely sustained by their atomic hardware. Or there is his essay on the American business guru James Burnham, author of *The Managerial Revolution*, in which, following Burnham, he prophesies a future of planned, centralised states, neither capitalist nor democratic, where, unlike the military empires of old, the shots are called by bureaucrats rather than soldiers. To this collection of try-outs and dry-runs can be added a third essay, 'Freedom and Happiness', again published in *Tribune*, which trumpets his discovery of Evgeny Zamyatin's clandestinely-published *We*, a satire of the Soviet Union, here disguised as 'Utopia', a 26th-century state run by a sinister entity known as the 'Benefactor', supported by a band of enforcers called the 'Guardians' and in which the shadows of Big Brother, the Inner Party and the Thought Police loom up ominously out of the murk.

As for the way in which Orwell was able to draw on work already filed and tease out some of its implication for the projects on which he was currently embarked, it is worth drawing attention to the pivotal role in *Nineteen Eighty-Four*'s long gestation played by 'Politics and the English Language', commissioned towards the end of 1945 by the magazine *Contact* but eventually published in Cyril Connolly's *Horizon* in April 1946. To understand what Orwell is up to in this account of the debasement of language for political ends it is necessary to go back to his pre-war novel *Coming Up for Air* (1939) and a scene in which the hero, George Bowling, attends a meeting of the West Bletchley Left Book Club. The visiting lecturer, bald-headed and intent, and introduced to the audience as 'a well-known anti-fascist', is an effective speaker, Bowling decides, but the dogged, repetitive style of his delivery makes him sound 'just like a gramophone record.' Come the end of the lecture, he is merely 'shouting out slogans' and prefabricated phrases. The very first cliché that catches Bowling's ear is 'bestial atrocities'.

Seven years later, in 'Politics and the English Language', Orwell returns to the curiously automated quality of modern political discourse. When you sit in the audience at a political meeting, he maintains, the suspicion that you are not watching a flesh-and-blood human being 'becomes stronger at moments when the light catches the speaker's spectacles and turns them into blank discs which seem to have no eyes behind them'. Clearly, this has something to do with the harangues of the West Bletchley Left Book Club and, we may infer, a lecture at which Orwell himself had been present. But Orwell, it turns out, has not yet finished with either the essay or the novel. On one level there is an obvious connection between the argument of 'Politics and the English Language' and 'Newspeak', the bleakly reductive formal code of Oceania. But *Nineteen Eighty-Four* also harbours an incident in which Winston, from a vantage point in the Ministry of Truth's canteen, watches a senior official from the Fiction Department deep in discussion with a female underling.

D. J. TAYLOR

Sure enough, 'his spectacles caught the light and presented to Winston two blank discs instead of eyes.'

There are several retrospective twitches of this kind in *Nineteen Eighty-Four*: look-backs to the life Orwell had been living and the people who populated it that go back ten or even fifteen years ('Bumstead J', who turns up at the Ministry of Love in the line of prisoners awaiting interrogation, is a reference to a grocer whom Orwell had known back in the Suffolk town of Southwold in the 1930s.) But if the Orwell who sat typing the final version of the novel in his study at Barnhill, as the paraffin heater pulsed at his side and the clouds of cigarette smoke rose over his head, was determined to put extra material of this sort into it, then he was also keen to take certain other kinds of material out. Several passages that exist in the manuscript failed to make it into the printed book. They include a horrifying scene in the propaganda movie that Winston watches in the prole cinema, in which the lynching of a black woman concludes with the desecration of her aborted child, and a description of the journey which precedes Winston and Julia's meeting at O'Brien's flat.

Yet in terms of the novel's plot, and the motivation of its characters, the most significant excision is a scene in which Winston and Julia come across each other after leaving the flat. Bidding farewell to his ladylove, Winston is oppressed by 'a curious feeling that although the purpose for which she had waited was to arrange another meeting, the embrace she had given him was intended as some kind of good-bye'. Orwell scholars have argued for decades about Julia's precise role in *Nineteen Eighty-Four* and exactly how she regards the distinctly unappetising older man with whom she begins a relationship. Here, the implication is that Julia is a honey-trap, tasked by O'Brien with the job of seducing Winston, confirming his political deviancy and inaugurating the long-drawn-out process that leads to his interrogation, torture and reeducation, before moving on to her next victim. Clearly, Orwell thought that in this passage he had gone too far.

There are other moments in which we can see Orwell censoring himself on grounds of possible racial prejudice or taste. An 'old fat Jew' strafed by machine guns as he tries desperately to swim away from a burning ship in the propaganda film is re-invented as 'huge great fat man', and the cache of pornographic photos of Winston and Julia making love that surfaces at the Ministry of Love is quietly deleted. All this returns us to the wider context of the half-decade or so in which *Nineteen Eighty-Four* was conceived and coaxed painstakingly into being. For all the care lavished on it, the multiple drafts and the tide of journalism that flowed alongside, the result still seems slightly unfinished. Several critics have noted the bright and well-nigh hallucinogenic quality that hangs over much of the writing and may have had something to do with Orwell's physical state when he wrote it. Orwell himself, a notoriously exacting judge of his own work, thought that it was 'a good idea' that he had failed properly to bring off. This is a harsh assessment. *Nineteen Eighty-Four* is one of the great dystopian novels of the modern age. But there is a suspicion that had Orwell lived, had more time, less distraction and better health – all the conditions that every writer who sets pen to paper struggles to achieve – the finished version would have been yet more different still..

NOTE ON THE CONTRIBUTOR

D.J. Taylor's *Orwell: The Life* won the 2003 Whitbread Biography Prize. *Orwell: The New Life*, a new biography which makes use of the wide range of sources which have come to light since that time, will be published in 2023. He is also the author of *The Prose Factory: Literary Life in England Since 1918* (2016) and *Lost Girls: Love, War and Literature 1939-1951* (2019). His most recent book is a volume of short stories, *Stewkey Blues* (2022)

ARTICLE

Some Thoughts on Manuscripts – with Particular Reference to *Nineteen Eighty-Four*

Richard Young

If you happen to want a copy of Orwell's *Nineteen Eighty-Four*, then you can go down to your local bookshop or order a copy online. It is in print and readily available.

Some people (me included) are not satisfied with this and want to have a first edition, for the rather odd reason of wanting to have this world-changing book in the form in which it first appeared back in 1949.

A first edition of *Nineteen Eighty-Four* (or any other book) is not actually the form in which the novel first existed. To get to publication there would have been various other stages. So occasionally that is why something known as a 'proof copy' may turn up.

Proofs were, and are, used by publishers and authors for making final changes and corrections to books just prior to publication. Sometimes (and certainly in more modern times), they have also been used for promotional and review purposes.

The proof for *Nineteen Eighty-Four* is a valuable and rare thing, though not particularly aesthetically pleasing. Essentially it is the text of the published novel in some rather drab blue wrappers, usually with the title handwritten on the front in ink. It contains little that is different from the final published text, though famously the title page gives the title as *1984* rather than *Nineteen Eighty-Four*.

Even this proof stage is, however, not truly the first appearance of the text. For that, one must go back to the author's manuscript.

George Orwell manuscripts are a bit of a problem, though, in that in virtually all cases they have not survived in any shape or form. In the case of *Nineteen Eighty-Four*, however, part of the manuscript has survived, and that provides a relevant case study on the allure of manuscripts generally. This is particularly so as a new facsimile edition of the *Nineteen Eighty-Four* manuscript has recently been published[1] though, in fact, an annotated facsimile was first produced by the great Orwell scholar, Peter Davison, some forty years ago.

The facsimile compiled by Davison actually shows that (as is typical) there were several stages of manuscript development prior to the production of final typescripts (and the final typescripts for both *Nineteen Eighty-Four* and *Animal Farm* can be accessed in the Orwell Archive).

The Davison *Nineteen Eighty-Four* manuscript facsimile edition reproduces surviving pages from four stages of preliminary drafts, much of it handwritten, though some of it typed with handwritten changes and corrections. A casual glance at many of the pages shows what seems often like an impenetrable mess. So it is no mean feat that Peter Davison with his annotations was able to summon order out of seeming chaos.

If proof copies tend not to be aesthetically very pleasing, manuscripts are often even less so. Manuscripts, however, (even incomplete ones like *Nineteen Eighty-Four*, representing around 44 per cent of the final published novel) are invaluable in helping to trace the development of a novel, and can provide insight into the creative process which simply is not possible from any other source.

They may show the author's original ideas for key passages, and how they were improved and refined. This is something that can clearly be seen even in the changes to the first paragraph of *Nineteen Eighty-Four* shown in the facsimile edition, where Orwell continued to refine the description of Winston Smith's arrival at Victory Mansions as the clocks strike thirteen on that bright cold April day.

Because of their rarity and literary importance, the original manuscripts of major novels such as *Nineteen Eighty-Four* are highly prized and valued. The original manuscript for *Nineteen Eighty-Four* now resides at Brown University, in the United States, after going through several ownership changes since Orwell's widow, Sonia, put it into a charity auction in 1952.

Most collectors have next to zero chance now of owning the surviving manuscripts by classic authors, most of which reside in academic institutions or museums. General manuscript material may be more attainable, however. By that I mean usually notebooks or original letters by authors, rather than drafts of their literary masterpieces.

Letters by famous authors like Orwell do occasionally turn up for sale. They can provide an unrivalled opportunity to own something touched by the author whilst also offering special insights into their life or creative process. Letters by an author which are handwritten, rather than typed, are usually preferred because of the more direct connection implied by handwritten, as opposed to typewritten, material (notwithstanding that they may be harder to read!).

RICHARD YOUNG

That latter comment does, though, beg an important question for our time. In a world where increasingly everyone uses a computer rather than putting pen to paper, or bashing away at a typewriter, what then will be the value of manuscripts in the future? How much, for instance, would you be prepared to pay for a PDF file your favourite modern author sent to their publisher? Just a thought.

NOTE

[1] *1984, Manuscript*, SP Books, Éditions des Saints Pères, 7, rue Pasteur, 14340 Cambremer, France; ISBN: 9791095457114; see https://www.spbooks.com/

ARTICLE

Big Brother Vladimir?

John Rodden ponders the whys and wherefores of yet another historic first for George Orwell's *Nineteen Eighty-Four*: topping the Russian bestseller lists in the winter of 2022-2023. Rodden pursues a seemingly simple question: is this news *doubleplusgood* – or *doubleplusungood*? – and finds it to be a conundrum just as deceptively complicated to puzzle out as a Thought Police entrapment setup in Charrington's antique shop.

DONALD, VLADIMIR AND THE MINISTRY OF ALTERNATIVE FACTS?

In a development uncannily – or eerily – reminiscent of its astonishing rise a few winters earlier to the top of the U.S. bestseller lists as a result of comparisons between Big Brother and incoming President Donald J. Trump, George Orwell's *Nineteen Eighty-Four* was top again on the bestseller lists last winter. The circumstances are, however, even more bizarre and astounding than in 2017 (Rodden 2020).

Why? Because this time Orwell's novel is No. 1 in … Vladimir Putin's Russia.

Wait! *Nineteen Eighty-Four* is No. 1 in … PUTIN'S RUSSIA? Huh?

As suspect as it may seem to Western readers, an official bulletin on 13 December by TASS, the state news agency, announced that Orwell's dystopia had led the 2022 ebook sales totals in fiction on the platform *LitRes*, the state online bookseller. Within moments, headlines and broadcasts throughout the West blared the news. TASS also reported that *1984* – the numerical title (in Cyrillic) prevails in all Russian editions – stood as the second most popular download in any category (Price 2022).

As occurred in January 2017, when endless comparisons were advanced in the media and blogosphere between Oceania and Donald Trump's 'Amerika' – and between Orwellian Newspeak and Trumpian 'alternative facts' – Western critics have not been slow since December to point out the numerous similarities between Orwell's Ministry of Truth and Putin's puppet propagandists. For example, arguing that *1984* represents a picture of Russians' wintry discontents with their fate under Vladimir Putin's iron rule, Britain's

JOHN RODDEN

The Independent declared in December that it was hardly surprising that Orwell's vision 'about citizens living under an oppressive regime that is continuously engaged in senseless war has become the most-read book in Russia' (Sharma 2022; see also Sabarwal 2022).

Media alerts to the puzzling and surprising rise of *1984* to No. 1 in Russia were loud and immediate throughout the West. A columnist for *MailOnline*, the digital version of Britain's *Daily Mail*, noted that Orwell's novel, published in 1949 when the cult of Joseph Stalin was at its height in the communist world, 'was based on Stalin's Russia' and the 'comparisons … drawn with Putin' were inevitable because both tyrannical regimes were 'Orwellian', operating as if they represented a gloss on *1984*'s line: 'The Party told you to reject the evidence of your eyes and ears.' Lest the Russian populace imagine that 2 + 2 = 4, Kremlin broadcasts blare unceasingly that Russia did not attack Ukraine, does not occupy any Ukrainian territory (i.e., formerly 'Ukrainian' regions have been annexed by Russia and are now officially 'Russian'), and bears its neighbour no malice nor ill will. Mocking the worldwide consensus trance that Putin is attempting to induce, the *MailOnline* headline ran: 'The bestselling book in Putin's "dystopian" Russia? Why, George Orwell's dystopian novel *Nineteen Eighty-Four*, of course!' (Price 2022).

'THE BESTSELLING BOOK FOR THE RUSSIAN CHRISTMAS'?

The story of Orwell's surge in popularity – TASS announced that sales of *1984* had soared 45 per cent since the invasion of Ukraine in late February 2022 – was even bigger news on the European continent. (EFE 2022; see also Sassi 2022*)* 'Orwell's novel about repression bestseller in Russia,' headlined Portugal's online business news publication (*CE Financial News Portuguese* 2022). It noted that 'Kremlin propaganda' about the Russian army conducting 'no attacks on civilian targets, despite waves of bombings …. that left millions of people without heat or electricity in the middle of winter' seemed pure *doublethink* out of *1984*'s Oceania. 'The story of absurd wars and totalitarian governments is all the rage in Moscow,' trumpeted Turin's *La Stampa* on 18 December (*La Stampa* 2022). It noted, ironically, that the timing of the novel's record sales figures made it 'the best-selling book for the Russian Christmas'. Meanwhile, in *Ouest-France*, the national newspaper with the largest circulation in the Francophone world, Carole Grimaux, a Professor of Geopolitics at the University of Montpellier III and the founder of the Centre for Russian and Eastern Europe Research, noted that 'the book resonates with the authoritarian regime of Vladimir Putin. '… [I]t is a work that brings Russians back to the Soviet past, because of similarities between the fiction they read and the reality they live.' As such, Russian readers' current encounters with *1984* represent 'a return to their past to understand their present and their future' (Lamort 2022).

Meanwhile, across the Atlantic, *Fortune.com* addressed the similarities between *1984*'s Newspeak and the Putin regime's infringements on freedom of the press, with both Russian journalists forbidden to discuss the Russian military activities in Ukraine as a 'war' or 'invasion,' which must instead be euphemistically described as a 'special military operation' (Prakash 2022). *Noticias Financieras*, the online Latin American news service, drew attention in December to Orwell's status in the Stalinist past of Russia, during which he 'was listed as one of the writers most critical of the Soviet totalitarian system' and was 'banned in the USSR' (*Noticias Financieras* 2022a). Contending that *1984* showed a Putin who resembled an everlasting Big Brother bogeyman, the journalist pointed out that Putin 'amended' the Russian constitution three years ago to remove presidential term limits, whereby he is now eligible to remain in power until 2036. Commemorating 'the 73rd anniversary of his death' on 21 January, *Noticias Financieras* added that the 'imaginary future' projected by Orwell 'in which totalitarian governments monitor their inhabitants and manipulate information' was 'still relevant today', especially in Russia, where 'in December it topped the bestseller list' (*Noticias Financieras* 2023).

THOUGHTCRIME—OR THE THOUGHT POLICE?

In a development that bears an uncanny resemblance to the plot of *1984* – in which Winston and Julia believe that they are joining the dissident Brotherhood yet are, instead, being set up by a standard Thought Police sting operation against potential rebels – it remains unclear whether the surge in popularity of Orwell's novel in 2022-2023 is part of a protest against Big Brother or a propaganda manoeuvre organised by the Putin regime. Which is it? Thoughtcrime – or the Thought Police?

Is the sales popularity of *1984* driven by Russian opposition to the seemingly endless war in Ukraine, which Putin invaded a year ago last 24 February? Or do Russian readers feel so besieged by the West that they believe the Kremlin line that Orwell's *1984* represents an attack on the West? Does *The Times* of London's headline on 15 December — '*1984* is Russia's No. 1' – serve to acknowledge thousands of acts of mass 'thoughtcrime' committed by a version of the Brotherhood and their numerous sympathisers? Or has the Orwell boomlet been manufactured and orchestrated as part of a diabolical propaganda campaign by the Ministry of Truth in cooperation with the Thought Police? Plenty of evidence exists for both claims – as implausible as the latter notion may seem to Westerners.

ARTICLE

JOHN RODDEN

Let us first address the conventional wisdom, namely that Russians' growing opposition to Putin is responsible for *1984*'s sales surge. As the already-cited headlines in European and American publications suggest, that is the predominant Western view. It is seconded by numerous hopeful Russian émigrés in the West. They note that several Russian intellectuals who have emigrated (or escaped) to the West since the invasion have been jailed over the years for having denounced the Putin regime as 'Orwellian' and invoking comparisons with *1984*.

The Kremlin denies such claims. Nonetheless, one Russian protester, businessman Dimitri Siline, was giving out copies of *1984* in March 2022, just weeks after the war started. He had paid $1,500 for copies that he distributed – in March and another several hundred in April – in his own city of Ivanovo, northeast of Moscow, as well as in Moscow subway stations and parks. Noting the parallels between Orwell's Oceania and Putin's Russia, Siline explained in an interview originally published in *Le Monde*: 'I wanted to offer people the chance to read it, and to start to think about it seriously.' (Arrested and charged with 'discrediting the Russian armed forces', he was 'merely' fined and then released.) (Freeman 2022; *Moscow Times* 2022).

Moreover, scattered polls show that 'more than half of Russians now advocate peace negotiations with Ukraine', according to a December 13 report in an online Latin American financial news publication (*Noticias Financieras* 2022b). (Another bestseller since the early days of the Ukraine war is a collection of Tolstoy's pacifist writings under the title *I Cannot Be Silent* – which has the force of a Zolaesque *J'Accuse* for some Russian readers; see Rebón 2023). Weary-minded and frustrated Russians who long for peace are not a silent 'majority' – but a silent 'plurality' of citizens to be sure – and part of a rapidly burgeoning minority numbering in the millions who are starting to criticise openly 'Big Brother Vladimir' generally and the war in particular. These Russians are well aware that, in May 2022, the novel was banned in Belarus by Alexander Lukashenko, 'the Kremlin's iron ally', as *La Stampa* characterises him. Some observers believe that the surge of interest in *1984* may arise from a fear that Putin, too, may soon ban the novel. These observers argue that *1984* also became a bestseller in Belarus in 2020-2021, reflecting (and perhaps contributing to) the massive protests against President Lukashenko that resulted in a severe crackdown on free speech and other repressive state measures, including the banning of the novel.

Other Russian dissidents concur with the prevailing Western view that the novel's rise in sales in Russia is explainable by the simple fact that the parallels between Orwell's Oceania and Putin's

Russia are eerily inescapable. For instance, Vladimir Kara-Murza, a Russian opposition politician, wrote from his Moscow jail cell in December that documentaries, cultural programmes 'and even sports coverage' are 'filled with propaganda messages' *à la* Oceania. He compared the Kremlin's 'relentless pro-regime and pro-war messaging' to *1984*'s Two Minute Hates, except that 'in Vladimir Putin's Russia, televised hate goes on for hours'. Kremlin propaganda has been 'ramped up to unprecedented levels', with virtually all light entertainment on all stations 'scrapped' and Channel One, Russia's flagship station, now devoted exclusively to agitprop from 9 a.m. to 3 a.m. throughout the week. The propaganda features the rewriting of history, with both Russia and the long-defunct USSR cast as 'a noble and benevolent state' and the 'Empire of Good', in the phrase of a New Year's Eve broadcast. In the New Year's TV special, the Kremlin's historical rectification, noted Kara-Murza, presented the USSR as 'destroyed by a mischievous scheme' of 'domestic traitors' in league with Ronald Reagan. (Let me remind readers that Reagan famously characterised the USSR as the 'Evil Empire'.) (Kara-Murza 2023).

Kara-Murza has been imprisoned in Moscow since April for speaking out against the war on Ukraine and is officially recognised as a prisoner of conscience by Amnesty International. He concluded his desperate message to Western readers:

> The leitmotifs are always the same: Russia is surrounded by enemies. The West seeks to humiliate and dismember it. The Soviet Union was a noble and benevolent state – 'the Empire of Good', as chief TV propagandist Dmitry Kiselyov put it … the only reason Russia still exists is because Putin is there to protect it (ibid).

In his frequent contributions to the *Washington Post* and other Western publications, Kara-Murza has argued that an international tribunal should be organised to address the Putin regime's war crimes – 'in the same way Nazi propagandists were tried at Nuremberg' – and 'the likes of' alleged Putin puppets such as Kiselyov and Margarita Simonyan (head of the state-controlled TV network RT [Russia Today]) 'should be brought to justice' (ibid).

'IGNORANCE IS STRENGTH'?

Lest you imagine that *Nineteen Eighty-Four* mirrors Russian life today, the Kremlin begs – and bowdlerises – to differ. I believe that the sales rise of the novel owes not only to popular discontent with Putin but also to Russian propaganda. After all, TASS has no qualms about publicising Orwell's bestsellerdom – as if to acknowledge that it is proud of its effective promotional campaign with the Russian public. Moreover, a half-dozen editions sold in Russian bookstores

JOHN RODDEN

and by *LitRes* and other online sellers – all of them are official editions translated and introduced by officially approved writers. Their prefaces specifically argue that the novel is about 'Western decadence', as the translator Darya Tselovalnikova, phrases it in a popular edition issued in May 2022. She omits any mention of parallels between Oceania and Russia, but rather argues that today's 'liberal totalitarianism of the West' closely corresponds to Orwell's nightmarish vision. According to Tselovalnikova, it is not Russia but rather the corrupted, 'liberal' so-called democracies of the West that are truly totalitarian in 2022 – that is, dominated by demagogues and vulgar populists who manipulate their nationalistic ('America First') demonstrations against Russia for their nefarious geopolitical purposes. 'Orwell could not have dreamt in his worst nightmares that the era of "liberal totalitarianism" or "totalitarian liberalism" would come in the West, and that people – separate, rather isolated individuals – would behave like a raging herd' (Price 2022; Bennetts 2022a).

It warrants emphasis that Tselovalnikova's edition of *1984* is the one that is selling on *LitRes* – and that has been aggressively promoted by the Russian media. His preface echoes the talking points of various Kremlin-sponsored cultural institutes, such as the Russian Strategic Culture Foundation (RSCF) and the Ministry of Foreign Affairs (MFA). For instance, the RSCF has published more than 200 articles that refer to Orwell's critique of the West. One contributor contends: 'I think it is safe to say that Orwell intended Big Brother to symbolise the British Empire, the largest empire that has ever existed in world history' (Ольга Юркова 2020).

Meanwhile, MFA spokeswoman Maria Zakharova has been insisting for at least a half-dozen years that *Nineteen Eighty-Four* mirrors the West. (She embarrassed herself in May 2017, in her first public reference to Orwell, when she dismissed reports about Russian meddling in American electoral politics as follows (ibid): 'This is pure disinformation – just as in Orwell's *1982*.'). 'Kremlin goes "Orwellian" on Orwell,' jeered Zakharova's critics (ibid) – though, of course, neither Zakharova nor they were aware that Orwell had, indeed, considered that title, along with *1980* and *The Last Man in Europe* – before choosing *Nineteen Eighty-Four* (Or rather *1984*, as his American publishers re-titled it.)

Asked in May 2022 at a public briefing 'what Russians should tell their relatives and friends in the West who maintain that *1984* mirrors Russia today', Zakharova repeated her line about Western disinformation and advised them to insist that any claims of similarities between *1984* and Russia were 'false'. Then she immediately shifted ground and went on the offensive, calling *1984* a looking glass for Western liberalism's 'unfreedom' of thought and castigating Western media 'propagandists'. Indeed, Zakharova has long reserved her sharpest vitriol for her colleagues in the Western media, lashing out above all at the 'doublethink' and 'Newspeak' of the duckspeaking American media, which she has characterised for years, even long before the Ukraine invasion, as 'shameful' exhibits of 'media vandalism':

> What U.S. and other media write is an attempt at total disinformation of … the global public, but the main target is the American public. First we called this a disinformation campaign. And then we changed the tone and described it as hysterics. But it is even worse than that, it's George Orwell's *1984*. We see now what he meant when he wrote about Big Brother. The Big Brother in the United States today is the U.S. media, which have moved far beyond the limits of professional ethics and competence and feel free to denounce and condemn, or simply to fabricate news. This is exactly what is happening now. This is terrible, because the heat of internal political competition has reached the media, including the U.S. media, which have joined the hostilities and are destroying the prestige and trust in media publications not only of their own public but also the international community as a whole (*Embassy of Russia News* 2017).

Not a word in this March 2017 statement about any possible relationship between *1984* and Russia – or in any subsequent official statements. In a press release issued in May 2022 and obviously timed to coincide with the publication of the new translation, Zakharova elaborated further, speaking in language that made even clearer that Tselovalnikova's slant on *1984* followed the Kremlin line. 'For many years we thought Orwell was describing totalitarianism,' she declared. That post-Gorbachev era of self-disgust and gullible acceptance of the West's denigration of the USSR represented a surrender to Western propaganda. Such a view of *1984* 'is one of the global fakes', she noted. 'Orwell wrote about the end of liberalism. He wrote how liberalism would lead humanity into a dead end.' Ignoring the obvious fact that most of the satirical references in *1984* address events and personalities (including Stalin as Big Brother) in the USSR of the 1940s, Zakharova concluded that Orwell 'wasn't writing about the Soviet Union, but about the society in which he lived' (*Moscow Times* 2022).

Zakharova's line on *1984* is repeated by a stable of dependable mouthpieces endorsed by the Ministry of Culture, along with members of the Russian parliament and Putin's political colleagues. Deputy foreign minister Sergei Ryabkov declared in a January 2023 interview with *RIA Gazeta* that it is 'pointless' to open negotiations for peace with 'Ukronazis' and 'their puppeteers'. Like many top

ARTICLE

JOHN RODDEN

Russian political figures, he exhibits a surprising knowledge of Orwell's coinages and their ubiquity in the propaganda wars (Vasilyeva 2022). He told *RIA Gazeta*:

> There have been a lot of direct quotes from Orwell in the statements of both American and NATO representatives. 'Peace Is War' is literally what is said every day from high tribunes and high offices in the West (cited in *Russian News*).

'Russia's actions in Ukraine are, in essence, anti-war,' Dmitry Kiselyov, the previously mentioned Kremlin TV host, has declared. Sergey Lavrov, head of the Foreign Ministry, has repeatedly denied that Russia 'invaded' Ukraine, duckspeaking the official line that Ukraine is a 'brotherland' that must be brought back into the 'Russian world' – a euphemism favoured by Vladimir Putin to rationalise and defend Kremlin domination of its sphere of influence and expansionist campaigns (Bennetts 2022b).

As the war began in 2022, Anatoli Wasserman, a deputy of Vladimir Putin's United Russia Party and formerly Russian TV's top current affairs pundit, told *Moscow News* that 'everything Orwell wrote about was his own experience at the BBC', where he served as a broadcaster during the Second World War. The setting in *1984*, said Wasserman, was Orwell's London – the capital of Airstrip One, the post-apocalyptic Britain – not Moscow nor any city in Russia. Why? Because Orwell was determined to expose the pretensions and lies of the West's so-called liberal democracies, which were – and remain – the real despotisms. The issue is not, therefore, Kremlin cant but rather White House whitewashing (see Feuillebois 2022).

Similarly, Yelena Panina, formerly a member of the Duma's foreign affairs committee, rechristened YouTube as the Ministry of Truth on account of its alleged anti-Russian biases and anti-Putin cancel culture policies. Panina also derided the German Foreign Ministry's decision to remove all Russia-sponsored channels and news archives from the internet, which she termed an historical rectification worthy of Minitrue drones that will 'deprive Germans of their [true] history' (Bennetts and Moody 2021).

BACK IN THE USSR?

However unlikely or even preposterous it may seem to Westerners that Putin's puppets are orchestrating a sales campaign to promote *1984*, it warrants emphasis that Putin's propagandists are not the first Kremlin mouthpieces to recognise the novel's potential propaganda value – and to claim that Orwell's novel is actually about the West. As long ago as the late 1950s, the cultural bureaucrats of the post-Stalin era were publishing articles about Orwell's 'satire of the West'. From the early Cold War era through the *glasnost* era under Mikhail Gorbachev in the late 1980s (when Soviet readers first encountered Orwell in an official translation), the Kremlin has sought to portray *1984* as a capitalist nightmare. For instance, in a 1959 article ('Under the hood of Mr Hoover'), a Soviet critic cleverly recast *1984* into a portrait of the American future in which the power of 'the Hoovers ... has reached fabulous heights'. The following year, *Kommunist* told readers that the secret affair of Winston and Julia really did make them guilty of sexcrime and typified 'the amorality which flourishes in some strata of bourgeois society, ... the growth of all kinds of temporary extramarital and family relations and open prostitution' (Kharchev 1960). A quarter century later, just as the West was crazed by 'Orwellmania' as New Year's Day 1984 approached, the Soviet press under Yuri Andropov, Putin's erstwhile boss in the KGB, greeted the arrival of the title year with the reminder that Orwell was, indeed, a visionary – about the global dominance of American imperialism under 'Big Brother Reagan'. As the Soviet daily, *Izvestia*, stated in a 14 January 1984 article:

> Every year from 1949 to 1984 made it clearer and clearer that Orwell, unwittingly or unknowingly (one could argue the latter), had painted not a caricature of socialism and communism, but a quite realistic picture of contemporary capitalism-imperialism (Sturua 1984).

Even in Gorbachev's USSR, the May 1988 introduction to the novel's appearance in *Literaturnaya Gazeta* spun *1984* via doublethinking dialectics into a critique of how 'Hate Week' was everyday Islam and 'the totalitarian shadowing of the population by means of the newest electronic equipment' was 'a reality precisely in the advanced countries of the West, most of all America' (Zalygin 1988).[1]

Is Putin's recourse to 'westernising' Orwell's *1984* simply a case of dusting off a tried-and-tested propaganda strategy from the Soviet era? A case of 'Back in the USSR'?[2]

As we can see, the main differences between the Soviet and Putin eras regarding *1984* are not the interpretations – Putin's anti-Western 'line' on Orwell is a direct echo of that of decades ago – but rather Putin's insight that he can exploit the novel by putting copies of the book in readers' hands, which the Soviets never dared to do until shortly before the USSR's collapse in 1991. Under Communist Party leaders ranging from Nikita Khrushchev to Leonid Brezhnev to Andropov, Party newspapers ran headlines about America's 'nuclear Newspeak' (e.g., Reagan's 'Peacekeeper missiles' stationed in West Germany), the FBI/CIA 'Thought Police' and the hapless impoverished 'proles' under capitalism – yet Orwell's novel was proscribed. The headlines and the sound bites referring to *1984* were everywhere. Yet the novel itself was nowhere to be found – officially,

JOHN RODDEN

at least. You could not buy it in a bookstore. You could not find it in a library. You knew little or nothing about its plot or characters. Yet you knew all its infamous coinages – because you had read and heard them in the state media. And perhaps you heard more – from the whispers of acquaintances who had somehow acquired a copy. For *1984* could only be read as *samizdat* – that is, as a 'forbidden' book passed on surreptitiously from person to person through the dissident underground. (During my travels in Eastern Europe in the 1980s, I found that many working-class, non-Party citizens knew the catchwords of *1984* – for the sole reason that the state media applied them to the leaders and institutions of the West.)

Although these hoary Soviet-era arguments about *1984* are long-standing, therefore, it is only recently that they have been taken up by Russian politicians – obviously as a result of the novel's bestsellerdom. Its rise to No. 1 may seem sudden. Yet Orwell's novel has been a big seller in Russia for more than a decade – though this December was the first time that its popularity was reported in the Western media. A Russian studies scholar at the University of Strasbourg, Victoire Feuillebois, wrote in a French magazine in June 2022 that *1984* had been 'a literary phenomenon as well as a political touchstone' in Russia for a dozen years (Feuillebois 2022). It sold approximately 1.8 million copies between 2009 and 2019, according to a French press report – and broke into the Russian 'top ten' list in 2015.

Even before the bestselling edition, translated by Darya Tselovalnikova and sponsored by the Ministry of Culture, appeared in 2022, therefore, *1984* was well promoted by Russian presses. One source reports that the print run for 2021 numbered 482,600 copies – that is, even before the upswing in sales during 2022 amid the Ukrainian war. Within weeks after the war's start, bookstore sales were up 30 per cent and online sales had jumped 75 per cent – while sales increases in recent months have been ever higher (*Moscow Times* 2022).

Of course, it is also possible that – as Putin critics claim – growing public discontent with Putin's government is the main driver behind *1984*'s sales and that the typical Russian reader is not succumbing to Kremlin propaganda about Orwell's novel. They argue that Russians are reading the novel with awareness of its horrifying parallels to their lives – and simply ignoring (or even defying) the anti-Western prefaces and state agitprop. These voices also contend that, if this is so, the case of Belarus is pertinent: Putin may be tolerating *1984*'s popularity and readying for a crackdown that would include banning such books if a national protest campaign were to arise comparable to the demonstrations that led to repressive measures in 2020-2021 in Belarus.

On the other hand, *1984* is also being taught in government-approved literature classes at the university level, apparently in keeping with the official line parroted by the Ministry of Culture that the novel is anti-Western and anti-liberal, not anti-Soviet. Those who credit Putin with the savvy to exploit *1984* for his own purposes also note that many Russians may, indeed, believe the prefatory material – even if they are feeling a growing frustration with the drawn-out war. That is to say, Kremlin propaganda about the book is well suited to a paranoid public that has long viewed Russia as an isolated victim of the nefarious Western conspiracy against Mother Russia. From this angle, Orwell (along with writers ranging from Kafka and Huxley to Solzhenitsyn and Cormac McCarthy) is coopted as a dystopian precursor of 'liberpunk', a prominent new literary current in Putin's Russia with an ideological bent that is libertarian, conservative and Slavophile. Condemning hideously invasive Western bureaucracies and Western 'decadence' and 'liberal immorality', liberpunk projects various apocalyptic near-future scenarios whereby the 'soft', 'indulgent' labyrinthine capitalist world self-destructs or implodes.

BOOKS MATTER – NYET?

A third possible explanation, which I consider the most plausible (and perhaps the most depressing), also deserves consideration. Have Vladimir Putin and the Russian establishment calculated that a form of literary *glasnost* is quite permissible – because it is quite harmless? The conjecture cannot be easily dismissed: Formerly 'dangerous' books during the Soviet era such as *1984* are now available from the official state bookseller, promoted by the Ministry of Culture, reissued in new editions from leading state presses such as AST Publishers in Moscow, and taught in Russian universities because – unlike the case throughout the Soviet era – they apparently no longer pose a threat to a 'totalitarian' regime, 'liberal' or illiberal.

This opinion has been advanced by Orwell's Russian-language biographer, Masha Karp, a dissident émigré residing in London and the author of *George Orwell and Russia* (Bloomsbury 2023, forthcoming). In one passage in her book, Karp takes a line from 'The prevention of literature' (1946) – Orwell's most famous defence of freedom of thought and expression – and gives it a fresh accent. Orwell writes:

> The organised lying practised by totalitarian states is not, as is sometimes claimed, a temporary expedient of the same nature as military deception. It is something integral to totalitarianism, something that would still continue even if concentration camps and secret police forces had ceased to be necessary.

JOHN RODDEN

The 'key words' that apply to 2023 Russia, argues Karp, are 'had ceased to be necessary' (Karp 2023a: 253-254). In a personal communication, Karp added that 'concentration camps' and 'secret police forces', albeit in rather different (and more insidious, less immediately visible) form, are still with us. 'What has really ceased to be necessary is the censorship of books.' Observing that the print runs of most 'dangerous books' are usually small (under 5,000 copies), she, nonetheless, re-emphasises her main point: 'You can't imagine what wonderful books have been published in Russia in the last 20 years! It is only now, with this war, that they do not publish on the cover the names of the authors who left the country in protest against it, but before 24 February, everything … was published… [The Kremlin] realised that books were not so dangerous after all' (Karp 2023b).

I believe that Karp would also grant that our first two explanations for *1984*'s bestsellerdom contain partial truths. She estimated in a personal exchange that 20 per cent of the Russian populace – numbering about thirty million citizens – quietly stands against Putin to varying degrees of opposition and would like in certain ways to see Russia more 'Westernised'. (This does not equate to backing the West's positions and/or participation in the Ukraine war, she notes, for which there is still far less – and little public and vocal – support). She estimates, further, that at least 30 per cent of Russians are strong supporters of Putin, consisting of 'fascists, racists and Empire-worshippers'. She concludes: 'Half of the population can be turned this way and that way, depending on the media – whether it is state-controlled or free' (Karp 2023c).

MAKING ORWELL A REALITY

George Orwell and *1984* have had a long history of attracting courageous dissident voices who have heralded its author as a truthteller and have compared Oceania to Russia – under Putin as well as Stalin. Among the most outspoken over the years who have expressed admiration for the author of *1984* is the distinguished Russian sociologist and public intellectual Lev Gudkov. A trio of intrepid late dissidents during the USSR and post-Communist days – Andrei Sinyavsky, Vladimir Voinovich, Vladimir Bukovsky – were well known in the West as votaries of Orwell's work and as exemplars of moral courage and intellectual integrity. After the USSR's collapse, all of these men became vocal critics of re-emerging authoritarian trends in post-communist Russia and, except for Sinyavsky who died in 1997, of Vladimir Putin and his government's actions since his rise to the presidency in 1999.

The first week of October witnessed the most prominent recent example of what Masha Karp calls 'the ritual invocation of Orwell's name among members of the Russian intelligentsia' (Karp 2023d).

The occasion was the publication of an open letter connected with the announcement of the annual 2022 Anna Politkovskaya Prize, which is given in the name of a dissident investigative journalist murdered in October 2006 after protesting against the Chechnya war and publishing articles critical of the Putin regime. Last year's 'Letter to Anna' was written by the 80-year-old human rights and peace activist Svetlana Gannushkina, an erstwhile colleague who has spoken out loudly against Kremlin warmongering from the Chechnya campaign to the Ukraine invasion. In the course of both honouring her friend 'Anya' and condemning the Putin regime for making Oceania the daily reality of 140 million Russians, Gannushkina exalts Orwell as a kindred spirit and inspirational presence. She writes:

> It is not only people who are repressed, but words, too. You can end up in detention [in Putin's Russia] simply for uttering them.
> Do you remember, Anya, that Soviet-era catchphrase: 'We were born [according to Soviet propaganda] in order to make Kafka a reality?'
> We are now successfully making Orwell a reality.
> We, many of us, are ashamed, but the country will be different when we succeed in transforming this shame into something constructive and learning to take responsibility for what is being done in our name (Gannushkina 2022).

As the sales figures in Russia of Orwell's *1984* suggest, these two intrepid women and the brave staff of *Novaya Gazeta* (which is published in Moscow) are not alone in seeking to 'make Orwell a reality'. Whether *1984* continues to sell widely in Russia – or becomes the victim of a repressive backlash as has occurred in Belarus – two developments seem likely to continue. Kremlin propagandists will continue their doublespeaking, duckspeaking propaganda in order to manipulate information and control the media. Yet also, Putin critics will commit Orwellian thoughtcrime. Denouncing the Kremlin's suppression of dissent and political opposition, they will dare – anxieties about the prospect of a 'Belarus backlash' notwithstanding – to invoke the language and vision of *1984*.

NOTES

[1] I am grateful to my colleague Mark Elson for his help with translations from the Russian.
[2] On the USSR line towards *1984* during the Reagan-Thatcher era of the 1980s, see also Tsoppi (1983). I have discussed Orwell's reputation in the USSR and in post-Soviet Russia elsewhere, most notably in John Rodden, *The Politics of Literary Reputation: The Making and Claiming of 'St. George' Orwell* (New York, Oxford University Press, 1989), chapter 3 ('Enemy of mankind: The Soviet Union's Orwell'); and John Rodden, *Scenes from an Afterlife: The Legacy of George*

JOHN RODDEN *Orwell* (Wilmington: ISI Press, 2003), chapter 3 ('Glasnost, Gorby, and the strange case of Comrade Orwell').

REFERENCES

Bennetts, Marc (2022a) George Orwell's *1984* is Russian bestseller in year of new extremes for Kremlin propaganda, *Times*, 14 December. Available online (behind paywall) at https://www.thetimes.co.uk/article/george-orwells-1984-is-russian-bestseller-in-year-of-new-extremes-for-kremlin-propaganda-c5pwp2jx0

Bennetts, Marc (2022b) Orwell's *1984* is Russia's No 1, *Times*, 15 December

Bennetts, Marc and Moody, Oliver (2021) Putin declares media war after German block on 'fake news', *Times*, 30 September

CE Financial News Portuguese (2022) Orwell's novel about repression bestseller in Russia, 13 December

CE Noticias Financieras (2022a) George Orwell's *1984*: A reflection of Putin's Russia?, 11 July

CE Noticias Financieras (2022b) Orwell's *1984* tops ebook sales in Russia, 13 December

CE Noticias Financieras (2023) Orwell's watch, 21 January

EFE (Spanish news agency) (2022) Orwell's dystopian *1984* tops list of ebooks in Russia, 13 December

Embassy of Russia News (2017) Excerpts from the briefing by Foreign Ministry spokesperson, Maria Zakharova, 3 March

Feuillebois, Victoire (2022) *1984* de George Orwell: Quel miroir pour la Russie de l'ère Poutine? [*1984* by George Orwell: What mirror is it for the Putin era?], *The Conversation*, June. Available online at https://theconversation.com/1984-de-george-orwell-quel-miroir-pour-la-russie-de-lere-poutine-185439 Translated in the English-language version of *CE Noticias Financieras* (2022a) George Orwell's *1984*: A reflection of Putin's Russia?, 11 July

Freeman, Colin (2022) How Vladimir Putin turned Orwell's *1984* into a reality, *Daily Telegraph*, 31 May. Available online (behind paywall) at https://www.telegraph.co.uk/books/what-to-read/vladimir-putin-turned-orwells-1984-reality/

Gannushkina, Svetlana (2022) Making Orwell a reality, *Novaya Gazeta*, 7 October

Kara-Murza, Vladimir (2023) Russians are living in a distorted reality; frightening propaganda permeates every aspect of society, *Calgary Herald*, Alberta, 21 January

Karp, Masha (2023a, forthcoming) *George Orwell and Russia*, London: Bloomsbury

Karp, Masha (2023b) Personal communication, 23 January

Karp, Masha (2023c) Personal communication, 28 January

Karp, Masha (2023d) Personal communication, 2 February

Kharchev, A.A. (1960) The Soviet family now under communism, *Kommunist*, May 1960 p. 57 (translated in *Current Digest of the Soviet Press*, 22 July 1960 p. 10)

Lamort, Edouard (2022) Le roman *1984* de George Orwell est en tête des ventes de livres en Russie, voici pourquoi [George Orwell's *1984* novel tops Russian book sales, here's why], *Ouest-France*, 16 December

Moscow Times (2022) Explainer: How Orwell's *1984* looms large in wartime Russia, 25 May

Ольга Юркова (2020) The Kremlin goes Orwellian on Orwell, Newstex Blogs, StopFake.org, 15 July

Prakash, Prarthana (2022) George Orwell's dystopian novel '1984' about an autocratic regime that oppresses its citizens is now a bestseller in Russia, *Fortune.com*, 15 December. Available online (behind paywall) at https://fortune.com/2022/12/14/george-orwell-1984-book-bestseller-russia/

Price, Oliver (2022) The bestselling book in Putin's dystopian Russia? Why, George Orwell's dystopian novel *Nineteen Eighty-Four*, of course! *Daily Mail*, 14 December. Available online at https://www.dailymail.co.uk/news/article-11539587/amp/George-Orwells-dystopian-novel-Nineteen-Eighty-Four-bestseller-Putins-Russia.html

Rebón, Marta (2023) Putin's dystopia, *CE Noticias Financieras*, 22 February

Rodden, John (2020) *Becoming George Orwell: Life and Letters, Legend and Legacy*, Princeton: Princeton University Press

Russian News (2023) Situation in and around Ukraine, 30 January

Sabarwal, Harshit (2022) George Orwell's novel *1984*, banned in the Soviet Union until 1988, tops Russian bestseller list, *Independent*, 15 December

Sassi (2022) Livro *1984* de George Orwell, lidera lista dos mais vendidos na Rússia [The book, *1984*, tops the bestseller list in Russia], *Agencia Estado, O Estado de Sao Paulo*, 15 December

Sharma, Shweta (2022) *Nineteen Eighty-Four* tops Russia's bestsellers of 2022, *Independent*, 17 December

La Stampa (2022) *1984* di Orwell è il libro più venduto del Natale russo: a Mosca spopola la storia di guerre assurde e governi totalitari [*1984* is the bestselling book of Russian Christmas: The story of absurd wars and totalitarian governments is all the rage in Moscow], 18 December

Sturua, Melor (1984) An Orwellian America, *Izvestia*, 15 January (translated in *World Press Review*, March 1984 p. 53)

Tsoppi, Victor (1983) *1984*: Full circle, *New Times* (English edition), 22-24 December

Vasilyeva, Nataliya (2022) Russia claims George Orwell wasn't writing about totalitarianism in *1984* in bizarre defence of war, *Daily Telegraph*, 22 May. Available online (behind paywall) at https://www.telegraph.co.uk/world-news/2022/05/22/russia-claims-george-orwell-wasnt-writing-totalitarianism-1984/

Zalygin, Sergei (1988) Here's what the editor-in-chief of *Novy Mir* thinks about 1984, *Literaturnaya Gazeta*, 11 May p. 15

NOTE ON THE CONTRIBUTOR

John Rodden has taught at the University of Virginia and the University of Texas at Austin, among other universities. He is the author, most recently, of *George Orwell: Life and Letters, Legend and Legacy* (2020) and *The Intellectual Species: Evolution or Extinction* (2022). He can be reached at jgrodden1@gmail.com.

BOOK REVIEWS

Orwell in Cuba: How *1984* came to be Published in Castro's Twilight

Frédérick Lavoie

Translated by Donald Winkler

Talon Books, Vancouver, 2020

ISBN: 9781772012453 (pbk)

Orwell in Cuba is an account of Canadian writer Frédérick Lavoie's visits to Cuba in 2016 and 2017 when there were plans, since fulfilled, to publish a new Cuban edition of *Nineteen Eighty-Four*. It is not an account of the struggle to publish *Nineteen Eighty-Four* in Cuba. There was no struggle. On the contrary, the decision to publish was almost certainly either an official decision or, at the very least, a decision with which Cuban officialdom was in full agreement. Lavoie gives us every reason for thinking so, although he never quite gets to the bottom of who signed off on it. Nor was this the first Cuban edition of *Nineteen Eighty-Four*. Nor, remarkably, even the first in Fidel Castro's Cuba. That honour goes to the short-run edition put out in 1960 – the year after Castro's revolution – by the small Havana-based Librerías Unidas. And although the book was not, until now, particularly encouraged, neither was it completely prohibited. Lavoie recounts how, in 2005, Englishman John Pateman went to the José Martí Library in Havana to see if he could access Orwell's books, *Nineteen Eighty-Four* included, and found that he could do so without difficulty. Eleven years on, Lavoie tried the same experiment and obtained the same result. Moreover, outside the libraries, he discovered that the book had been circulating clandestinely and to a considerable readership.

This is in no way to imply that Cuba is an open and permissive society. Lavoie amply demonstrates that that is not the case, noting, among other things, the 75 dissenters arrested and imprisoned in the Black Spring of 2015; or the Ladies in White who rallied in their support despite official harassment; or the case of Oswaldo Payá, a Cuban political activist who died in suspicious circumstances in a car crash in July 2012. To this may be added the disgraceful treatment of the poet Heberto Padilla who was jailed on vague charges in 1971 and then made to read a public confession accusing himself and others of vaguely defined attitudes and activities contrary to

Castro's regime, or that of the writer Carlos Franqui whose fate was distinctly Orwellian – 'unpersonned' because he challenged Havana's support for the Soviet invasion of Czechoslovakia in 1968, written out of the official record and airbrushed from photographs ('I discover my photographic death – do I exist?' cited in Perrottet 2019: 345). And yet Orwell himself could be read there and in the public library, which was a surprise to me.

The Cuban revolution of 1959 brought Fidel Castro to power and established a regime that is, at the time of writing, still in place. It is the most enduring system of government Cuba has ever had. Although the island had been officially independent since the early 1900s, it had been, as Lavoie notes, politically and economically under American influence for all of that time. This included, initially at least, considerable restrictions on Cuba's ability to act independently, a permanent American military presence at Guantánamo and an understanding that the United States might intervene if it appeared that Cuba was slipping the Washington leash. The best-known American intervention in Cuba – the failed Bay of Pigs invasion of 1961 – was of this kind, initiated at the prospect that independent Cuba was beginning to act a great deal too independently and undertaken with the aim of bringing the country back under US control. Lavoie's researches in the archive reveal that the coming invasion was vehemently denied by the Kennedy administration right up until it was an undeniable fact. That it was repulsed greatly surprised most of its organisers. Strangely, Lavoie does not mention the subsequent, and well-regarded, analysis by psychologist Irving Janis (1972) which stressed that an important failing on the American side had been the dismissal, among the organisers, of sharp internal criticism at the planning stage. Janis named this 'groupthink' in conscious imitation of Orwell's Newspeak and as a warning of what might happen when conformity trumps intellectual rigour. (Unfortunately, naming the phenomenon has not ended it. Nor even slowed it up).

What is interesting about socialist Cuba is that it survived at all, and that it has survived so long, outliving the Soviet Union. Castro neither restored nor abolished Cuban democracy. How could he have restored or destroyed what there had been precious little of? In 1959, Cuba had been nominally independent for a little over half a century and had been formally democratic for a fraction of that time. After the revolution, several hundred political opponents were shot on the orders of the new government. But once the regime was in place and confident, the shootings largely stopped. Dissidents – the criteria for dissent being quite broad – were imprisoned, roughed up. Or, increasingly, they were exiled, which was neither commendable nor, given the vicinity, out of the ordinary. If, as I

BOOK REVIEW

think is the case, there is now less of that than there once was, that is obviously to the good.

However, the point at issue between Cuba and the United States was never human rights – the Americans had tolerated and sustained a great deal worse, in Cuba, and elsewhere. Cuba was attacked on account of its new assertiveness, which included its decision that, henceforth, a greater part of the country's wealth would benefit the poor instead of the rich at home and abroad. Castro's revolution aimed, primarily and unideologically, to address the basic inequalities in Cuban society. On that basis, there could have been friendly relations between the small, under-developed island and its superpower neighbour. Fidel Castro was more populist than communist at the start and may have remained so had he been handled differently. There seems little disagreement on that. Tony Perrottet, who is sympathetic to Castro, says so, but so does Anthony DePalma, who is not (DePalma 2020). Perrottet writes that Fidel's brother, Raúl, and Ernesto 'Che' Guevara were the communists, not Fidel himself, and that Cuba's Communist Party did not endorse him nor his movement, regarding him as 'a middle class dilettante' (Perrottet 2019: p. 133). Cuba became formally communist only following the Bay of Pigs whereupon it became the bugbear of successive American administrations, whale to their Ahab, Road Runner to Coyote.

It would have been unremarkable if *Nineteen Eighty-Four* had been banned in Cuba. In the high days of the Cold War, Cuba was a Soviet client state while *Nineteen Eighty-Four* had been written by a committed and eloquent opponent of Soviet communism and as a warning to any democratic socialists who might be tempted to go the Soviet way. It was for precisely that reason that it was taken up by the West and actively deployed as anti-Soviet propaganda. The US secretary of state, Dean Acheson, for example, described it, and *Animal Farm*, as assets in the 'psychological offensive against Communism', as Lavoie comments (p. 132). He, therefore, authorised the financial support for foreign publishers wishing to produce translations.

But Havana's Librerías Unidas does not appear to have been one of them. In the year or so that it operated, Librerías Unidas put out maybe a dozen titles, most of them, indeed, the standard Cold War reading list – *Nineteen Eighty-Four*, *Animal Farm*, Arthur Koestler's *Darkness at Noon* (1940), Milovan Djilas's *The New Class* (1957). But it also published a couple of books critical of American involvement in Latin America – Lavoie mentions *The Tragedy of American Diplomacy*, by William Appleman Williams (1959) and Juan José Arévalo's *The Shark and the Sardines* (1961). This mixed output makes him sceptical that the Havana publisher was backed by American government agencies for Cold War purposes. He reckons it was the private project of Adolfo Cacheiro Fernández, who ran a radical bookshop in Cuba's capital and had blown hot then cold on the Castro regime, eventually going into voluntary exile.

Revolutionary Cuba's attitude towards Orwell appears to have been that if you really had to read him, you could read him in the library, but if you wanted to read him outside the library, then you took your chances. Daniel Díaz Mantilla, a poet and editor, tells Lavoie that he first read *Nineteen Eighty-Four* in the late 1980s, a copy borrowed from a friend. And José Miguel, a prolific science fiction author, says he managed to obtain a copy in the nineties and found that he could read it reasonably openly. He was concerned at the time that being in possession of the book might get him into trouble with the authorities. But no trouble came of it. Cubans were apparently in the habit of making protective covers for their books and once a book had a cover on it, it was sufficiently anonymised so it could be read with reasonable confidence that the reader would be left alone. All in all, the status of *Nineteen Eighty-Four* seems to have been ambiguous. Nowhere was it officially spelt out that the book was banned (outside of the public libraries). Then again, nowhere was it officially said that it was permissible. It may be that what is not officially permitted is for all intents and purposes banned. But it is hardly much of a ban when it can be circumvented by putting a cover on the book and reading it discreetly. By way of contrast, I think it unlikely that anyone in the Soviet Union (aside from the KGB) could have read, say, Solzhenitsyn's *The Gulag Archipelago* (1958-1968) so long as they were moderately careful, and put an anonymising cover on it.

In 1930s Britain, Joyce's *Ulysses* (1922) and Henry Miller's *Tropic of Cancer* (1934) and *Tropic of Capricorn* (1939) were among the books officially prohibited on grounds of obscenity. No English press would touch them, and no shop would stock them, not openly anyway. But they were published abroad, in Paris, by Sylvia Beach's Shakespeare and Company and by Obelisk, and they could be obtained by mail order or by sneaking them through customs, with only a small risk of being caught.

Ulysses and the *Tropics* were among the prohibited books Orwell owned, several of which were seized when the police raided his house in August 1939. Some were later returned to him on the grounds that he was a literary man and that these were the kind of books a literary man might need to read. In 'Inside the Whale' (1940), he writes of those banned books in a way that makes clear that he has read them closely and he writes to readers who, if they have not already broken the law and read them too, might now feel inspired to go out and do so. It was not an ideal arrangement, that a person who wanted to read a work of literary merit with sexual content (or, for that matter, a book with sexual content and no literary merit whatsoever) had to go outside the law to do so and risk the shame of official chastisement should the law find out, but it was hardly repression. The high tide of Puritan intolerance had passed. Orwell had caught it at its ebb. That it was ebbing may not have been clear in 1940, but it would be obvious some two decades later when Penguin published D. H. Lawrence's *Lady Chatterley's Lover* and survived the subsequent obscenity trial. It is a story John Sutherland tells with style (Sutherland 1982).

I get the sense that the Cuban revolution has grown similarly lax in this, its middle age. From banning rock music to welcoming the Rolling Stones. From official atheism to three papal visits. How else to explain the *Paquete Semanal* (*The Weekly Package*), a hard-drive that does its clandestine rounds offering downloaded American TV shows, films and publications, all for one dollar-convertible peso? The access is illegal, the *paquete* is illegal, but the government turns a blind eye so long as what is distributed is not overtly political or, *plus ça change*, pornographic. From Lavoie's account, the Cubans appear short, not so much on culture, as on the more material treats of capitalism.

Thinking of doing Fabricio González Neira, the translator of the Cuban *Nineteen Eighty-Four*, a big favour, Lavoie writes: 'I'd proposed bringing to him from North America a book in English of his choosing. He replied that he already downloaded many more titles than he was able to read, but that, on the other hand, he'd be most grateful if I could buy him some chocolate, as he found the taste of what was available in Cuba to be "so to speak, naïve"' (p. 29).

This is the context in which the new Cuban edition of *Nineteen Eighty-Four* was sanctioned for publication. A great many Cubans had already read it and a great many more would likely do so whether in library copies, editions smuggled in from abroad or the bootleg digital versions circulating on datasticks. Indeed, the very fact that it was being so widely read may have been a factor in the decision to publish it properly.

Like many a socialist regime – all of them, in fact – Cuba has had to make its peace with market forces. Part of this coming to terms is that some of the country's publishing houses have been accorded business status – they receive a grant from the government but must cover some of their own costs from their revenues. Lavoie provides a fascinating account of the Cuban book business as it takes its first, unsteady steps to market. At the top of the hierarchy of Cuban publishing there is an Instituto Cubano del Libro (Cuban Book Institute) which mediates between the country's Ministry of Culture and its various publishing houses. The institute financially assists the publishers, sets the prices they can charge and vets what they can publish before publication. It is then up to the publisher to sell enough books to bridge the gap between the subvention and their costs. Arte y Literatura, the publisher of the new Cuban *Nineteen Eighty-Four*, is likely to do well out of it. The only risk that I can see is that it may be difficult to sell a book officially that has already done the rounds under cover. But, politically, the risk is surely nil. If unofficial circulation has not unsettled the regime, why should the official version?

It may be that Arte y Literatura itself decided that it wanted to publish *Nineteen Eighty-Four*. It would have been a shrewd commercial initiative, particularly once the work was out of copyright. Lavoie's contact at the Institute tells him that that was exactly how it was – publishers can publish what they like so long as it benefits society. But others say different – that it is unlikely that Arte y Literatura would have chosen to publish *Nineteen Eighty-Four* on its own initiative. The decision to publish could only have been taken by the institute or even the ministry. I wonder, though, if more of a fuss is being made here than is justified. Where a government, or one of its agencies, subsidises publishing, it is entirely normal that it then has some say in what is published, even if just for quality control. This is not unique to Cuba, or communism or even the left. Perhaps Arte y Literatura had the idea of publishing *Nineteen Eighty-Four* and it persuaded the Institute that it was a good idea to do. Or perhaps the ministry or the institute had the idea of publishing the book and that it then planted the idea in the publisher's head. However it was, it seems a small bureaucratic story.

That the Cuban *Nineteen Eighty-Four* has a preface at all is also unsurprising. These days, scarcely a book is published – no classic anyway – without a preface whose author tells us what they made of it. A recent Penguin edition of *Nineteen Eighty-Four*, for example, is introduced by Thomas Pynchon. Pynchon notes some frequently observed parallels between the contemporary United States and the fictional Oceania: 'News is whatever the government says it is, surveillance of ordinary citizens has entered the mainstream of police activity...' (Pynchon 2004: 16) and later says that it has become 'a commonplace circa 2003 for government employees to be paid more than most of the rest of us to debase history, trivialise truth and annihilate the past on a daily basis' (p. 22). Orwell, he writes, 'well before' 1939, regarded most of the British Labour Party

BOOK REVIEW

as 'potentially if not already fascist' and that 'more or less consciously he found an analogy between British Labour and the Communist Party under Stalin' since both were 'in reality concerned only with establishing and perpetuating their own power' (p. 10).

Orwell was concerned that *Animal Farm* and *Nineteen Eighty-Four* may be read as works hostile to socialism in all its forms. He had intended them to be read as hostile to one version of socialism only – the Soviet version – which was antithetical to the democratic version, of which he would remain a supporter to the end of his life. But when both works were taken up by Western governments during the Cold War, it was because of what they opposed. Orwell was the man who twice fictionalised a failed revolutionary socialism.

Yet because Orwell was a socialist, *Animal Farm* at least was not quite fit for Cold War purposes. In that book, the allegorised socialism functions as a productive system. The animals collectively work the farm more efficiently and more productively than Jones ever did. Not only that, but they successfully modernise it, achieving Snowball's ambitious plans for electrification. There is nothing in *Animal Farm* that says that socialism is an inherently flawed economic system. Even the actual Soviet famines of the 1930s are, in Orwell's allegory, depicted as propagandist myth. The revolution fails solely because the worst – the pigs – get to the top and the rest are easily persuaded that this is a good thing. *Nineteen Eighty-Four* makes for better Cold War propaganda in this respect because the worst are already in command. We see nothing of the revolution except what is in the bogus accounts put forward by the Party and the little Winston can remember. Based on these, it can be deduced that there was a revolution in 1940 or thereabouts (the same year Orwell himself believed Britain was in a revolutionary situation), that it took a dictatorial turn in the 1950s, and that the Big Brother faction took over around a decade later. There is no suggestion that socialism ever delivered. In *Nineteen Eighty-Four*, the London of the eighties remains the damaged city of immediate post-war years, dilapidated from years of neglect.

Lavoie finds the occasional parallel between Castro's Cuba and Orwellian dystopia. The Committees for the Defence of the Revolution, for instance – 'neighbourhood snoops' as Sarah Rainsford dubs them in her assured and balanced memoir, *Our Woman in Havana* (2018) – or Daniel Díaz Mantilla, whom he likens to Winston Smith on account of all his efforts in the archive to get a sense of pre-revolutionary life. There is also a poem, 'She and Bay and the Years,' which features approximately midway through the text and which offers a kind of history of the revolutionaries in government. Castro had initially wanted to break Cuba's economic dependence on the production and export of cane sugar, but within a few years his government was planning, instead, to up the sugar output to ten million tons a year. A *volte-face*, to be sure, but it is perhaps a stretch to liken it, as Lavoie does, to Napoleon in *Animal Farm* deciding that he supported the windmill project after all. A more charitable view may be that the about-turn on cane sugar was merely the belated recognition that a small economy dependent on a single commodity could not be diversified overnight, not when that dependence was built up over more than a century. A paradox of the Cuban condition around 1960 was that, on the road to diversification, it would need to produce in the short run a great deal more of the very thing it had become dependent on. That was its sole means of generating revenue. It is the problem many ex-colonies have faced if they push for economic independence.

Socialism aspires to a planned economy in which, given time, the planned product will match what is needed, and markets can be jettisoned. In practice, this pristine socialism of theory, the post-market world in which, as Orwell wrote, all goods could be made as cheap and as plentiful as tap water, has proven unattainable. The socialists of all parties are eventually drawn back to economics of the market and its institutions. The transition can be unnerving. Ambitious welfare states scaled down in the interest of global competitiveness, a competition many will lose. A widening inequality is soothed by the promise of eventual trickle down, if not now, then later. The Cuba Lavoie describes is somewhere on this curve, the governing elite – notably the army – acting as a kind of entrepreneur, while wary of actual small-scale business owners, the *cuentapropistas*, who may, in time (probably quite a long time) become rich and thereby independent of the state.

The commercial decision to publish *Nineteen Eighty-Four* is an aspect of Cuba's slow drift to the market. If *Orwell in Cuba* is primarily an investigation of that decision, it is also a fascinating look at the lives of ordinary Cubans caught up in this change. 'People are very poor here,' Roberto Torres, an economist cautiously sympathetic to the economic changes happening in Cuba, tells Lavoie. 'They're afraid to lose the very little they have.' Emilio, for example, a 62-year-old statistician who now faces an unexpectedly uncertain future. He may once have envisaged living out his life cared for by his country's remarkable system of socialised healthcare. Now, who can say? Free universal healthcare may, in time, be sacrificed to market forces. It would be bad news for Emilio were this to happen. The services that have been there pretty much his entire life may soon be gone, just as he reaches the age at which he will likely need them most. But others would gain. Medics, for instance. In Cuba, Lavoie comments, they are poorly paid by Western standards (less than 60 Canadian dollars a month). True,

BOOK REVIEW

they have perks such as free accommodation and no utility bills. But the new consumer products now available in Cuba such as smartphones and the internet are beyond their reach unless they are gifted them on the side by rich, grateful patients. They would be better off in the private sector if there were one or if one were to be brought into being. And they would be better off in the United States which, in 2006, on the initiative of the junior George Bush, financially induced them to come across, a mean-spirited ploy that has cost Cuba some 7,000 skilled people (Rainsford 2018: 178).

Lavoie wonders: were he to include the words 'I hate Castro' in *Orwell in Cuba,* would Cuba ban the book? Criticism is one thing. Cuba's officially sanctioned publishers publish criticism, but a declared hatred for the key figure of the revolution might prove a different matter. It would, the author decides, say something about Cuba if he were to put those very words in his book and the book get published in Cuba even so. I do not know if Lavoie's book ever did get published (or at least distributed) in Cuba, in translation, and with those words in it; if it made its way through the hierarchy of the island's publications industry and a decision taken that some of that industry's limited resources be allocated to putting it into circulation. I suspect not.

He has actually said those words, however. He read aloud: 'I hate Fidel Castro, I hate Raúl Castro' at the Havana International Book Fair on, splendid irony, Valentine's Day 2017. He does not, he says, really hate the Castros. But he does not like them. He is no admirer of their achievement; indeed, he would, I suspect, question that it was an achievement at all. They have done more harm than good, he says, but he can see that it would be bad if their system were to come down all in one go, suggesting it better that it crumble bit by bit.

'If I write,' he comments, 'it is to help ensure that in Cuba, as elsewhere, today like tomorrow, two and two continue to make four. And to arrive there, George Orwell has shown himself to be an excellent travelling companion' (p. 189). Elsewhere, Lavoie describes Orwell's Oceania as a place 'where reality is robbed of its indisputable existence' (p. 206). But no regime could do that – deny reality, demand that its citizens commit to a collective solipsism – and none has ever tried.

There is no dictatorship that has literally tried to deny a fact as blatant as two plus two equal four. Scepticism about truth, the idea that reality is socially constructed and so forth, was an affectation – usually Marxist in inspiration or in the general Marxist ballpark – of elite discourse in Western universities where it was sometimes seen as revolutionary, or potentially so. I suspect it has no potential whatsoever. A worldview that insists that there is no truth, no verifiable facts, is dead before it starts, instantly consumed by its own absurdity. On the other hand, the denial of particular truths – inconvenient truths – goes on all the time, and Cuba has no monopoly on it.

Lavoie says that, in *Nineteen Eighty-Four*, the Party holds that the historical record is endlessly mutable. He comments that Winston is 'unable to compare the present with the distant past' and must therefore accept the Party line that things have been getting better since the Revolution. For the purposes of *Nineteen Eighty-Four* as political fiction, it is important that Winston cannot remember much about the recent past and that no one he meets can do so either. There is a similar necessity in *Animal Farm* where, towards the story's end, the animals cannot recall if they were better or worse off before the revolution. But outside of fiction most people will have an opinion on the past versus the present and whether things are better or worse than they used to be. Frédérick Lavoie does not, I think, in the end, believe that a political system can control past, present and future to the extent that it can put itself beyond criticism, or that Cuba is such a system. In Cuba, there is an official view and a public critique and, going by Lavoie's account, it is the critique that seems to be making headway.

Are Cubans generally better off after the revolution? Compared with what? Compared with how they may have been if there had been no revolution? Or compared with how they may have been if the revolution had delivered all it said it would deliver? Cuba, under Batista, became a vicious police state that operated hand-in-glove with American organised crime and aped its methods. There was an economy based on foreign ownership of the island's principal assets, and tourism that specialised in providing visitors with the wickedness they could not so easily obtain at home. The revolution delivered health and educational services that were better and more equally distributed than in the pre-revolutionary period. And the country is more independent. Is it more democratic than before? Is it less? The revolution did not deliver all it promised and the revolutionaries have had to pull their horns in. Part of their problem, however, is that the United States will not trade with them. For sixty years, their superpower neighbour has operated what amounts to a blockade against them, one that has compounded the costs arising from the economic system they have chosen to implement. Lavoie may, I think, have commented more on this.

In Lavoie's view, the Cuban regime is trying to promote a particular version of reality, one with all the discreditable bits taken out. He writes of a 'five-decade archival gap in objective reality' (p. 206) in Cuba that will make it difficult in the future to assess the revolution, its achievements and its failures. But that kind of

BOOK REVIEW

assessment is never easy. Rising GDP may hide significant and widening income inequalities. Full employment can coexist with poor pay and conditions. People's romantic ideal of the past can distort how they read the present.

Orwell would have found much to interest him about post-revolutionary Cuba. The socialism it implemented was a form of economic order he may have recognised and welcomed as something like the system he proposed in *The Lion and the Unicorn* (1941) – the planned economy, the comprehensive nationalisation of production, the regular appeal to national solidarity, the use of rationing, the reinvention of currency as a kind of ration voucher, the approximate equality of income. Its lack of democracy would have affronted him, of course, as would the restrictions it has placed on free expression, and its treatment of some who went ahead and spoke their minds regardless. It may have surprised him, too, that it had failed to deliver, after more than sixty years, better material conditions, or at least some sign of them..

REFERENCES

DePalma, Anthony (2020) *The Cubans: Ordinary Lives in Extraordinary Times*, London: Viking

Janis, Irving (1972) *Victims of Groupthink: A Psychological Study of Foreign-Policy Decisions and Fiascoes*, Boston: Houghton, Mifflin

Perrottet, Tony (2019) *Cuba Libre – Che, Fidel and the Improbable Revolution that Changed History,* New York: Blue Rider Press

Pynchon, Thomas (2004) Introduction, *Nineteen Eighty-Four,* New York: Penguin pp 8-26

Rainsford, Sarah (2018) *Our Woman in Havana: Reporting Castro's Cuba,* London: Oneworld

Sutherland, John (1982) *Offensive Literature: Decensorship in Britain, 1960-82,* London: Junction Books

Martin Tyrrell,
Queen's University, Belfast

The Radio Front: The BBC and the Propaganda War 1939-45

Ron Bateman

Cheltenham, Gloucestershire: The History Press, 2022 pp 256

ISBN: 9780750996648

Published during the BBC's centenary year, this book tells the story of the corporation's growth and successes during the Second World War and its contribution to winning it. Over 256 pages this is not going to be comprehensive academic history, but it has a compelling focus on the crucial role of positive propaganda in the fighting of the war.

Ron Bateman is one of the founding members of the thriving Orwell Society, Orwell's son, Richard Blair, writes the Foreword and Dione Venables, now in her nineties and the founding chair of the society, writes a memorable Introduction. In this, she highlights the important place of BBC radio in her life when she was a child growing up in those momentous years of invasion threat, blitz, total war on the Home Front, the invasion of Europe and eventual victory. She offers a poignant account of the peril she and hundreds of thousands of teenage children experienced between 1939 and 1945.

She remembers her mother crying and her father close to tears when they gathered around their radio set in their suburban living room to hear Neville Chamberlain declare war on Germany on the first Sunday of September 1939. She recalls being forever haunted by being withdrawn at the last minute from the transatlantic trip on the *City of Benares* to Canada in 1940. Her parents could not bear to be without her and her sister. Her luggage, including her most beloved toys, went down with the ship which was torpedoed by a German U-boat in the middle of a convoy. Dione was so fortunate not to be among the 83 of the 90 children evacuees on board who drowned (p. 13).

In 1944, she would also survive being buried in the wreckage of her home outside Beckenham after a V1 doodlebug landed in their garden. She also remembers hearing over the radio the evocative sound of a disabled girl singing 'When the lights go on again, all over the world; And our boys are home again, all over the world' from Piccadilly Circus on VE Day, 8 May 1945 (p. 16).

Orwell worked for the BBC between 1941 and 1943 writing, producing and broadcasting what would now be regarded as 'soft propaganda' to listeners in British India. He was a journalist and author famously dedicated to communicating truth, but gave up two years of his writing and creative life to propagandise through

BOOK REVIEW

broadcasting for patriotic purposes. It was a messy compromise. Great Britain was fighting for survival and for its Empire which Orwell had come to despise. But as the majority of Indians accepted at the time, it was better to fight for British imperialists who were more likely to agree eventually to independence than for Japanese imperialists who had demonstrated in China and elsewhere in the Pacific that they offered genocide and a subjugation much more terrible. Indeed, the British Indian Army of more than two and a half million was a volunteer army which fought bravely and courageously throughout the world with Indian soldiers winning 30 Victoria Crosses.

Richard Blair touches on the irony that one of the BBC's most reluctant propagandists, who left the corporation thinking he had achieved virtually nothing and had condemned the BBC as a cross between a lunatic asylum and a girl's school, now has a statue commemorating him in front of Broadcasting House and bearing one of his iconic maxims: 'If liberty means anything at all, it means the right to tell people what they do not want to hear' (p. 7). I suspect George Orwell, today, would be chuckling at the paradox, and at the same time deeply moved that his son and admirers of his contribution to literature and journalism should have campaigned so successfully to remember him in this way.

It is also true that the BBC tolerates a monument to a writer who satirised it so viciously in *Nineteen Eighty-Four* with Room 101 (based on a BBC location where he worked) being the place where Winston Smith is tortured and the Ministry of Truth (based on the BBC's wartime overseer, the Ministry of Information, located in the new Senate House headquarters of the University of London) being the spreader of lies and falsified history.

As Ron Bateman explains, the BBC's war effort combined traditional British amateurism, disorganisation and unpreparedness together with brilliant improvisation once the full media and military threat of the Axis powers became apparent. The assistant director of programme planning, Harman Grisewood, returned from a grim tour of Nazi Germany in 1939 to report to the BBC's second director-general, Sir Frederick Ogilvie, about the dangers of Hitler's regime. Ogilvie regarded the Germans as 'a very sentimental people' who could be moved by a rendition of Beatrice Harrison playing her cello to the sound of the singing nightingale (p. 20). Ogilvie clearly missed the trick for this was a fabricated stunt. Nightingales never sang in Berkeley Square according to the lyrics of the hit song penned by the BBC's *Radio Times* editor and later head of variety, Eric Maschwitz. And they did not respond to Beatrice Harrison's playing. The so-called live broadcast from a wood in Surrey was, in fact, a bird impressionist simulating the nightingale combined with Beatrice playing 'Londonderry Air' on her cello. What mattered here was the illusion of broadcasting magic, persuasion through emotion, and a dash of what Winston Churchill said was 'the protection of democracy with a bodyguard of lies'.

Ron Bateman places Orwell's wartime propaganda stint in impressive context. In the first chapter, he tells of John Reith, the corporation's first director general 'who successfully negotiated a significant measure of independence for the BBC – a hard-won argument that held firm until the General Strike of 1926 when he was strong-armed by Whitehall into denying striking workers and their unions a voice over the airwaves' (p. 18). Reith resigned from the BBC in June 1938 (p. 19) and lasted only two years in various ministerial roles between 1940 and 1942 being inevitably defenestrated given the longstanding antipathy and dislike Churchill and he had for each other.

Chapter Two concentrates in detail on the BBC's preparations for war – such as the setting up of the Monitoring Service in 1939. Originally based at Wood Norton in Worcestershire, it aimed to counter the propaganda of German and Italian broadcasters. 'By 1941 over 400 monitors of various nationalities were listening in for twenty-four hours a day, requiring over a million spoken words to be carefully assessed and condensed into a single document to be scrutinised for inconsistencies by the various Overseas Service directors' (p. 35).

In Chapter Three, titled 'Not The War We Expected', Bateman highlights the extraordinary apathy of many during the first months of the war. 'On the evening of 27 May 1940, at a time when the BEF was hemmed in at Dunkirk and Britain could potentially have been invaded at any moment, Orwell went with his wife to a local pub to hear the evening news. The barmaid had no intention of turning the radio on, and when she finally relented, he observed that nobody else in the room bothered to listen' (p. 60).

The next chapter examines the important role the American journalist, Ed Murrow, played in the Allies' propaganda campaign. 'Murrow's motivation was to capture the reality and the deeper meaning of the Blitz over London, effectively "putting America's ear to the pavement". Both *London After Dark* and its sister programme *London Carries On* not only found a regular slot on CBC and NBC but also across a whole network of mutual broadcasting systems' (p. 83). Such was Murrow's importance that Churchill considered him a personal friend.

The ethical dilemmas of purporting to win trust while at the same time broadcasting with the purpose of influencing the attitudes of listeners on the home front and those in occupied territories is covered in a chapter titled 'Crossing the Propaganda Line' while in 'Talking to Europe' Bateman investigates how the BBC became a voice of hope for oppressed peoples trapped in Nazi Germany's fortress of Europe. He then concentrates on country and regional case histories – covering Vichy France in Chapter Ten and broadcasting to the German-speaking populations in Chapter Eleven. The next chapter deals with the ways in which the BBC sought to win the hearts and minds of the colonies, particularly students and educated elites through the Eastern Service where Orwell worked for two years. The epilogue summarises the BBC's strategy and impact during the invasion of North West Europe in 1944 and how the policy and content of the programming changed during the period which ended with military victory.

This is a fascinating history of broadcasting weaving details of incidents and events which were fundamental to the BBC's development as an effective warrior of the airwaves. For example, Lawrence Gilliam's innovative blending of fiction and actuality in the nine-part series charting the rise of Adolf Hitler and the Nazis, titled *Shadow of the Swastika*, achieved audience figures of up to 12 million between 1939 and 1940 (p. 54). But this ethically problematic genre of BBC features using dramatisation to depict true events led to serious errors with the representation of the Battle of Narvik in Norway in the spring of 1940. The depiction of a Chief Stoker as a survivor when he had, in fact, been killed caused great distress to his family, and the widow of an officer who also died in the battle wrote to *The Times* to condemn the BBC for the unpardonable sin of impersonating the voices of the living and the dead (pp 55-56).

Ron Bateman also provides an overview of Orwell's frustrations and achievements during his time as a BBC producer. It seems he was a willing part of the propaganda machine, but at the same time succeeded in playing the game his way with some cunning. As a result, he was able to engage his creative, cultural and educational instincts in organising a kind of war-time Open University of the Air largely targeted at Indian left-wing intellectuals. Of course, Orwell did not in the least bit mind that many of them were most probably bitterly anti-British since the 'intention was not to "fox the Indian Masses"; rather it was to present an awareness of what a fascist victory would mean to the chances of India's independence' (p. 219).

The author captures the mischief in Orwell's method with 'his penchant towards organising broadcasts on the subject of prison literature, at a time when India's future leaders including Gandhi and Nehru were in prison' (p. 221). And while the Ministry of Information frowned upon putting in front of the microphone certain Indian intellectuals and political activists, Orwell gladly booked them on the basis of their literary merit.

The Radio Front is a comprehensive and readable account of the BBC's propaganda campaigns. Bateman shows how both Orwell and the BBC managed to do some good and his statue and the BBC's current headquarters stand rather well together in commemorating that legacy.

Tim Crook,
Goldsmiths, University of London

George Orwell

Subscription information

Each volume contains two issues, published half-yearly.

Annual Subscription (including postage)

Personal Subscription

UK	£39
Europe	£43
RoW	£45

Institutional Subscription

UK	£100
Europe	£115
RoW	£120

Single Issue copies can be purchased (subject to availability)

Enquiries regarding subscriptions and orders should be sent to:

> Journals Fulfilment Department
> Abramis Academic
> ASK House
> Northgate Avenue
> Bury St Edmunds
> Suffolk, IP32 6BB
> UK

Tel: +44(0)1284 717884
Email: info@abramis.co.uk

www.ingramcontent.com/pod-product-compliance
Lightning Source LLC
Chambersburg PA
CBHW080438230426
43662CB00015B/2311